THE
FREEDOM
FIGHTER

THE FREEDOM FIGHTER

The Amazing Story of **WILLIAM ~ WILBERFORCE**

DERICK BINGHAM

CHRISTIAN FOCUS

© copyright 1998 Derick Bingham
reprinted 1999, 2002
ISBN: 1-85792-371-5
published by Christian Focus Publications Ltd.
Geanies House, Fearn, Tain, Ross-shire, IV20
1TW, Scotland, Great Britain.
www.christianfocus.com

Cover illustration by Nick Mountain
Allied artists

Printed and bound in Great Britain by Cox and
Wyman Ltd, Reading, Berkshire

Contents

AUTHOR'S NOTE

This is a true story. All the events actually took place. The more important conversations are based on what people really did say at the time. The less important conversations, and some background details are imagined.

'This book is dedicated to the
Lord Blease of Cromac
whose selfless work for so many people
in the House of Lords is deeply
appreciated and who showed deep
interest in the preparation and
publication of this book.'

'Oh Lord Jesus,' she
prayed, 'How long
shall I suffer this way?'
Mrs Henson
Slave

INTRODUCTION

'No! No!' cried the little boy, 'Please No! I want to stay with my Mother!'

'Be quiet!' shouted the man, callously pulling his mother away from him. She was taken to a raised platform and offered for sale, immediately.

Described on the 'Slaves at Sale' notice as 'A very superior washer, ironer, cook and house woman' the interest among the slave owners in buying her was intense.

'100 guineas, sir, I see you,' cried the auctioneer. 'Any advance on 100?'

'120, 130... yes 140! Any advance on 140? Yes, 150, sir, and more, 160?'

On and on they continued, a coarse looking slave owner bidding higher and higher. His name was Isaac Riley.

'200? Any advance on 200? Is this the highest bid? Am I bid any more? No more bids, then, gentlemen? This is a trusty, intelligent and excellent worker - freely guaranteed. Is 200 the last offer? Right, then, going, going, gone to Mr. Isaac Riley.'

'Now, let's have the boy,' cried the auctioneer, motioning for the slave's terrified son to be led up to the huge platform. 'Josiah Henson. A very fit and good-looking five year old male. What am I bid for him?'

'A tough little urchin,' whispered one of the slave owners, 'He would make a good house-boy.'

'I'd keep him for picking cotton myself,' said another.

A number of men were interested in buying the child and the bidding was brisk.

Standing in the crowd watching the proceedings, a surprised Isaac Riley felt hands suddenly gripping his knees. Josiah's mother had pushed through the crowd and had fallen at his feet.

'Please, Mr. Riley, please buy my boy!' Mrs. Henson pleaded. 'All the rest of my children are sold and I plead with you to buy him so that we will not be separated. You can afford it, sir, surely you can! Please let me have just one of my children!'

'And just who do you think you are?' replied Riley furiously.

'The child's mother, sir, that's all!' she replied. 'If you have children of your own, sir, you will well understand how I feel. Would you like to be separated from any one of them? I will work for you, sir, I will serve you well, I promise, but just let me have my boy.'

'I'll let you have this!' replied Riley who started to mercilessly kick Mrs. Henson. She fell from his knees groaning and tried to roll away from him, but he came after her, beating her with violent blows.

'My child! Please, my child!' screamed Mrs. Henson.

'I'll not buy your child,' cried Riley, 'And that's an end of it!'

Weeping with the intense pain he had inflicted, Mrs. Henson began to crawl away on her hands and knees. Yet, as she moved, she was heard to sob a prayer to the Lord.

'Oh Lord Jesus,' she prayed, 'How long shall I suffer this way?'

* * * * *

Millions of African men, women and children suffered a similar kind of fate in the 18th and 19th centuries. The British, the Americans, the French, and the Dutch were particularly deeply involved in the

11

slave trade. They bought another human being in the same way as we might buy a cat or a dog.

In one year alone 185 ships took 43,755 people from Africa by force. Many were flushed out by slave traders who burned their villages. They were marched to the coast with huge yokes around their necks to prevent their escape. On board ship many perished in the fearful conditions below deck. Those who survived were then faced with the likes of Isaac Riley as their master.

Had God heard Mrs. Henson? Where would the answer to her prayer come from? Who would dare to rise up and condemn the disgraceful practice of slavery and seek to destroy it? Where would slaves find a friend?

An important part of the answer to her prayer was to come with the birth of a boy on August 24th, 1759. His name was William Wilberforce, and he was to become one of the greatest friends of slaves that ever lived. Here is his amazing story.

'Oh!, I'd love to be a sea captain,' thought William, 'and then I could explore the countries of the world!'

A letter from a schoolboy

'Here he comes!' cried the excited crowd. Everybody strained to catch a glimpse of their thin, bearded King as he rode his large horse down the main street of Hull.

'He's smaller than I thought,' a lady commented to a friend as he passed.

'Not so small that he can't raise a huge army,' said another, 'and my husband will be called up to serve in it, I warrant!'

The retinue of accompanying horsemen reined in at a large, red bricked house on the main street. No. 27, belonged to the Lord Mayor, Sir John Lister, who stood waiting for King Charles II at the gate.

'Welcome to Hull, your Majesty. And welcome to our home.'

'It's a pleasure to be here, Sir John,' came the reply, 'and what a fine house you have here.'

King Charles spent the night at the Lister home, and ate in a banqueting room with oak-panelled walls bearing the Lister coat-of-arms above the fireplace.

In this famous house, now open to the public, William Wilberforce was born. Outside, the back garden ran to a steep bank of the River Hull , and at high tide William would watch ships sail up and down. At low tide, barges were pulled or punted from one large warehouse to another. Hull was the fourth port of England after London, Bristol and Liverpool.

'I wonder what St Petersburg is like?' William thought one day as he watched a Russian ship go past the family garden, the name of its port written clearly on its bow. Another day a ship from Sweden came past, heavily laden with iron ore.

'I'd love to go to Sweden,' thought William. Many a time he would stand and watch the ships being loaded with everything from ponies brought in from all over the countryside to knives from Sheffield.

'Oh! I'd love to be a sea captain,' thought William, 'and then I could explore the countries of the world!' His grandfather, who had been Mayor of Hull, had become a very rich merchant through owning ships and trading with the Baltic. William's father, Robert, became a managing partner in William's grandfather's business and he also became a very wealthy and successful merchant.

God had great plans for Robert's little boy but his becoming a sea captain was not one of them.

One day William, now seven years of age, came charging through the front door of his home, through the large hall, tiled with black and white squares like a great giant chess board, and up the main wide staircase to his sister, Sarah's room.

'Sarah! Sarah,' he cried, bursting into the room.

Sarah looked across to her fair haired brother who stood before her in his full skirted coat, knee-breeches, white stockings and buckled shoes.

'Sarah, you'll never guess. Mr Milner, our teacher, swung me onto the table in front of the whole class today. He made me read from the book, *Robinson Crusoe* for about five minutes.

"There," cried Mr Milner, pointing with one of his hands to me and with his other to my class, "That's how you all should read!"'

'But you do have a lovely voice!' replied Sarah, at which her brother burst out laughing.

* * * *

She was, of course, absolutely right. William's voice was to become one of his most famous qualities. One day he would become one of the greatest speakers in history and be named, 'The Nightingale of the House of Commons'. The house on High Street was often to ring with the lively cries of Robert and Elizabeth Wilberforce's son, for he was a little bundle of energy as well as having a very bright mind.

Sadly, though, little William's life was soon to be filled with sorrow.

Running upstairs one day, just home from the Grammar School of Kingston-upon-Hull, his mother Elizabeth came out of her bedroom looking very sad.

'William, you must not make a noise,' she said, closing the door gently behind her, 'Your father has taken very ill.'

William stopped in his tracks, feeling numb.

'How ill, Mother?' he asked.

'You can come in to see him, but you must be very, very quiet,' said his mother gently.

William would never forget his father lying in that room so very ill.

'You must be good to your mother and Sarah,' he kept saying.

William failed to recognise that death was not far away.

When his father died there was no sadder boy in all of Hull than William Wilberforce. He stood by his father's graveside, a heartbroken lad of nine amongst the mourners.

'God bless you son!' the various merchant-friends of his father's said to him as they shook his hand. They all wondered what would become of him.

His Uncle William came up to the young boy's mother.

'You must let him come and stay with us in Surrey, Elizabeth,' he said gently. 'Hannah and I have no children of our own. We will be more than happy to have him with us at Wimbledon. He is a delightful child, and besides, it will bring relief to you at this very difficult time.'

'It's very good of you, William,' replied Mrs. Wilberforce, 'I'll bring him to you next year. It won't be easy for him to leave Hull, but it will be for the best.'

'There will be plenty for him to do,' assured William's uncle. 'We'll send him to school at Putney and he can also come and stay at our London home at St James' Place.'

One year after his father's death, a carriage pulled up at No. 27.

The various servants stood at the gate as the coachman began to load up the luggage. Lots of tears were shed and William received many hugs and kisses.

'We'll miss you lad,' said the cook who had fed William so often when he would sneak into the kitchen, ravenous for food! She didn't know what she was going to do without him. Sarah, perhaps, was the most heartbroken of all.

'Write soon, William,' she said through her tears, 'Tell me all about London.'

'I will,' he replied 'and will you please write to me and tell me what's happening at home?'

'I promise,' said Sarah as William and his mother were helped by the footman into the carriage.

'Forward!' cried the coachman as the horses started over the cobbled stones and William Wilberforce started out on the first of many long journeys in his life from Yorkshire to London.

The distance to London was 175 miles and the coach could only cover 30 per day. William and his mother had to stay at various inns on their journey.

'What's the coachman carrying pistols for, Mother?' asked William when they got out at the first inn.

'I'm sorry I have to tell you,' replied the lady, 'but there are many dangerous highwaymen about who hold up coaches and rob travellers!'

'Will we be robbed?' asked William.

'Please God, we won't,' said his mother trying to reassure her little boy whose eyes were now filled with fear.

Their journey went well, and William was fascinated by all the different scenes that passed before his eyes. As they travelled across the rolling English countryside passing towns and villages, he began to wonder what on earth London would look like. Soon they arrived in Nottingham and immediately William was on the lookout for Robin Hood and his Merry Men.

'Do you think we'll see any of them?' he asked, enthusiastically.

'I'm afraid not,' replied Mrs. Wilberforce, 'They have long since died. Though, what fun we had, reading all those stories about them, didn't we? I think you liked Maid Marion best!'

Soon the coach began to near the great city of London. At an inn, one evening, as they were eating their meal, a nearby traveller began to tell the story of what had happened the night before.

'Ah! It was a very grizzly affair, Ma'am. The stagecoach was passing through Epping Forest when it was attacked by no less than seven highwaymen.'

'Seven!' cried William, 'They must have been determined to rob the travellers.'

'They certainly were lad,' replied the traveller, 'but the guard was very brave. He killed three of them before he was killed himself.'

No-one was happier to get safely to London than William.

At last the coach brought them to Wimbledon and his uncle and aunt. After a short stay, his mother returned to Yorkshire and left William to settle down into his new surroundings. He later described his school as 'a most wretched little place' where 'they taught everything and nothing.'

He particularly detested the school dinners and when he grew older he stated he could remember 'meals which I could not eat without sickness'.

The one great thing in William's life,

though, was his love for his uncle and aunt. He had not lived with them for very long before he discovered that they both had a deep love for the Lord Jesus and were very enthusiastic Christians. They were friends with one of the best known Christians in England, the Rev George Whitfield. Although William did not realise it at the time, Whitfield was to go down in history as one of the greatest preachers in the history of the Christian church.

Whitfield had a great friend called Rev John Wesley who was to become the founder of the Methodist Church. Wesley was equally as famous as Whitfield, and Hannah, William's aunt, had come to know the Lord Jesus as her Saviour through his preaching. William was often taken along to church services.

'Who is that little boy who sings with such a beautiful voice?' people began to say. They could not help but notice the little boy's voice which soared above the singing of the congregation at services he attended.

John Wesley's brother, Charles, had written hundreds of new hymns, and William soon got to know and love some of these songs of praise.

There was one minister, though, who probably deeply influenced the little boy more than all the others.

This minister had once been a captain of a ship bringing slaves from Africa to the West Indies and had been converted to Christ in the middle of a thunderstorm in the Atlantic Ocean. Now he was a Church of England minister at Olney in Buckinghamshire. William thought the world of John Newton and loved his stories and his sermons.

John Newton was a man who was full of fun and had a very affectionate nature, and as a child, William treated him almost as his father. Little was the ex-sea captain and slave trader to realise the influence that his sermons were soon to have upon the boy and the world of slavery.

When William's mother heard of his interest in what he was hearing at the church services he attended, she was determined to put a stop to it all.

Although she went to church herself she was against anybody showing great 'enthusiasm'. She brought William home to Hull to get him away from the spiritual influences that were shaping his mind and heart. William later wrote, 'Being removed from my uncle and aunt affected me most seriously. It almost broke my heart, I was so much attached to them.'

The headmaster of William's old school had also turned with enthusiasm to the Gospel, so Elizabeth sent William to a school in a town called Polkington, thirteen miles from Hull.

If you visit the Holy Trinity Parish Church in Kingston-upon-Hull, you will find, above the entry to the tower stairs, in the north east pier, a marble monument to the Rev Joseph Milner, who was, for thirty years, headmaster of the Grammar School and a leader of the Evangelical Revival. William was later to become a very prominent leader himself in this Revival, though his mother would never have dreamed it could have happened.

William lived in the house of his new headmaster and soon became a very popular boy in the school. He had a great gift for mimicry and would "take off" the voices and mannerisms of his teachers. His friends would urge him to mimic their teachers and they fell about with laughter whenever he did.

He was very fond of poetry and used to learn it just for fun. When he went for a walk he usually carried a book of poetry in his pocket!

One day, when William was fourteen years old, he handed a letter to a friend of his called Walmsley.

'Please would you post this for me on your way home?' asked William.

Walmsley many years later, recalled how he saw that the envelope was addressed to the Editor of a Yorkshire newspaper and he was very curious.

'What on earth is the letter about?' he asked.

'It's a protest against what I have called, "The Odious Traffic in Human Flesh," answered William enthusiastically.

'And what, may I ask, is "The Odious Traffic in Human Flesh"?' enquired a very surprised Walmsley.

'You'll see, if the Editor publishes it,' said William with a smile.

Soon millions were to see what lay in the heart of the lad from Hull.

'Possessed of great charm,
Wilberforce was amusing, quick
witted and had a good singing voice.'
Geoffrey Hanks,
Seventy Great Christians

To Cambridge

In the history of Cambridge University there have been few students more fun-loving, winsome and popular, than the 17 year old William Wilberforce who became a student there in 1776.

'Ah! Cookson,' said William dashing around St John's College one morning, 'I'm having a crowd to my room this evening for a party. Will you join us?'

'As long as you have that legendary Yorkshire pie of yours!' replied his friend.

'I promise you that there will be lots of it,' said the hazel-eyed, five foot four inch Wilberforce, as he dashed on to his morning lecture.

'Christian!' said Wilberforce hailing another student in the corridor. 'My rooms tonight for a party? Yes? Around seven?'

'I suppose I will have to listen to your

songs!' said Edward Christian whose brother Fletcher later lead the famous mutiny on the *HMS Bounty* in the South Seas.

William was now a very wealthy young man because, through the deaths of his grandfather, his father and his uncle, he had been left a lot of money.

His mother was the guardian of his fortune and he was told that he could, more or less, do what he liked. He certainly had plenty of money to spend on whatever he pleased.

As it turned out, William liked to entertain. He loved to have students round to his rooms where his wit and sense of humour had everybody laughing. He loved singing and listening to instrumental music.

That evening, as darkness began to fall, a crowd of jostling, joking students were found to be heading for Wilberforce's rooms.

They had brought with them a fellow student who had never met Wilberforce before. He was very different in personality and while Wilberforce wasted a lot of his time, away playing cards and entertaining his friends, this student was very studious and was also rather shy.

'What a pie!' chorused the hungry

students as they tucked into the food Wilberforce had provided.

'It won't last long at this rate!' said Thomas Gisborne who had rooms next door.

Soon, William was called across the crowded room to greet his new guest.

'Allow me to introduce William Pitt,' said one of Wilberforce's fellow students.

'Pleased to meet you Pitt,' said Wilberforce, 'I hope they have introduced you to my Yorkshire pie.'

'First class food!' said the quiet Pitt, with a smile, as Wilberforce poured him a drink.

'And what area of study are you interested in?' asked Wilberforce.

'Astronomy, Greek and Roman literature, mathematics, Shakespeare and law,' replied Pitt.

'Goodness,' said Wilberforce, whose love of study was less than fervent, 'and what do you hope to do with all of that?'

'I hope to follow my father, the Earl of Chatham into the British House of Commons as a Member of Parliament,' said Pitt, laughing.

That night, in St John's College, a friendship began between William Pitt and William Wilberforce which was to last for the rest of their lives and was to influence millions of people.

Life at Cambridge University was filled with action for the lively Wilberforce. Even those who taught him at University liked his company and sometimes invited him to play cards with them.

'Their object,' Wilberforce later wrote, 'seemed to be to make and keep me idle. If ever I appeared studious they would say to me, "Why in the world should a man of your fortune trouble yourself with study?"'

Unfortunately Wilberforce listened to them and he did idle a lot of his time away when he should have been attending lectures.

'Well, if it isn't young Wilberforce!' shouted a familiar voice.

William stopped in his tracks. It was Isaac Milner, his former schoolmaster at Hull Grammar School. It was the man who had set him on the desk and made him read *Robinson Crusoe* to his class.

'Mr Milner!' said Wilberforce in surprise, 'What on earth are you doing at Cambridge?'

'I am a student here,' said Milner, 'believe it or not.' As it turned out Milner not only proved to be a brilliant student but he was later to become the Vice-

Chancellor of the University and to play a very important part in leading William to a personal knowledge of the Lord Jesus as his Saviour.

'I reckon you are reading more than *Robinson Crusoe* now, Wilberforce!' said Milner with a laugh.

'Maybe I should be reading a lot more than I am,' replied William, feeling rather guilty about his neglected studies.

Even his friend, Thomas Gisborne, who had rooms next door to him used to tell how when he was getting ready to go to bed he was called by Wilberforce making music on his poker and tongs as their chimneys were back to back.

'Come on, Gisborne, let's talk,' Wilberforce would shout.

'It was a dangerous thing to do,' Gisborne wrote later, 'For his amusing conversation was sure to keep me up so late that I was behind next morning with my work.'

A lot of history surrounded Wilberforce during his three years at Cambridge University. Even his own College, St John's, had been founded as far back as 1511.

The great Bible scholar Erasmus attended Cambridge as did Sir Isaac Newton who later discovered the law of gravity. William, despite his lack of dedication to intensive study, fortunately never had to be dealt with by the University proctors. These men were appointed for a year at a time and went through the streets of Cambridge, at night, with private constables known as 'bulldogs' dealing with unruly students.

The proctors had the power to send a student down from Cambridge for good or 'gate him' (make him stay in College after dinner) or simply fine him.

Even with the presence of proctors, life at Cambridge University has never been dull and the high spirits of students through centuries has been legendary. Despite this, the high standard of scholarship and achievement out of Cambridge University has been equally legendary and it has long been one of the greatest Universities in the world.

After three years at Cambridge, William took and passed his final examinations. The results were not brilliant and were a reflection of the time he had wasted in social activities. His life was now at a crossroads.

Yet, despite Wilberforce's love of fun, his friends knew very well that there was a serious man in the making. His friend

Gisborne actually said that Wilberforce was 'by far the most agreeable and popular man among the undergraduates of Cambridge.'

Now that he had graduated, though, his life was at a crossroads. What career was he to choose? Three possibilities lay before him. He could idle his life away looking for pleasure. He could enter a life of business, or, he could enter a life of helping people by public service.

Pleasure had left him very unsatisfied and the business in Hull, from which he drew his money, was managed for him by his cousin. The third possibility of a life of public service actually appealed to him most. During his final year at Cambridge, in the winter of 1779-80, Wilberforce had spent a great deal of time in London, much of it in the Strangers Gallery of the House of Commons.

Often he was joined by his friend William Pitt. The Gallery was provided for anyone who wanted to observe Parliament in action.

The two friends talked a lot about what they saw.

'Things are really lively here at the moment,' said William one evening as they watched the Members of Parliament in their white wigs with rich velvet coats of bright colours and lace ruffles and satin knee-breeches. 'This American War of Independence is causing a lot of discussion.'

'I hear we are now being defeated on land and sea since the French and Spanish have entered this war,' answered Pitt. 'It doesn't look good for us.'

The scene at the House of Commons in those days was quite different from today. The House of Commons gathered in a disused chapel called St Stephen's in Westminster, on the banks of the River Thames.

Inside were three rows of seats facing each other. The Government supporters sat on the right of the Speaker and the Opposition on the left. It was the Speaker's duty to keep order when Members of Parliament were constantly trying to shout each other down. There were six hundred and thirteen members in a very badly overcrowded house.

The building was burned down in 1834, and the present Palace of Westminster where the House of Commons now gathers, was begun.

'Let's go to *Goostree's!*' said Pitt after watching a long and very lively debate in the House of Commons.

This club, called *Goostree's* was in Pall Mall where Pitt and Wilberforce often ate. Night after night the two men would gather there with about thirty of their friends and talk about politics.

* * * *

In May, 1780, William Pitt told his friends he had decided to stand as a Member of Parliament representing Cambridge University.

'And what about you, Wilberforce?' somebody asked.

'I am going to stand for Hull, my native town,' said Wilberforce, and the very next morning, set off for home.

All that summer Wilberforce worked furiously, encouraging people to vote for him in the coming election. He began to speak at large meetings and tell people his views on all sorts of issues. He discovered that he had great power over his audiences.

Though Parliamentary candidates were often pelted with rotten eggs and cabbages when they spoke at political meetings, Wilberforce discovered that his audiences actually laughed at his jokes and applauded him enthusiastically. He also had very quick and clever answers to all the questions that were asked of him.

In those days it was the custom of a Parliamentary candidate to bribe those who voted for him. Each elector was usually paid a guinea and the landlord of a local inn was told to give them free food and drink at the candidate's expense. As William had a large fortune he was able to pay a guinea to a lot of electors. He spent nearly eight thousand pounds on the election. Today, that would amount to nearly one quarter of a million pounds.

On August 24th, 1780, William was given a tremendous 21st birthday party by his mother. People from all across Hull and district were invited to come and share in the festivities. In a field near his home an ox was roasted and a huge crowd enjoyed the party.

'If you give us parties like this every year, William, we will vote for you for a life time!' said one reveller to Wilberforce. 'Happy birthday to you,' the crowd sang enthusiastically as the roasted meat was eaten and the drink flowed.

'Bravo, little Wilberforce,' they shouted. 'You are our man in Parliament for Hull.'

'With your help I'll make it,' said William and he did.

* * * *

On September 12th the result of the Parliamentary election for Hull was declared at the Guildhall. Wilberforce won the election by a huge margin and he and the opponent nearest to him were elected as the two Members of Parliament for Hull.

He received one thousand, one hundred and twenty-six votes which was exactly the same number that his two opponents had between them! He was on his way.

Meanwhile, all over the world, slaves continued to be bought and sold and treated disgracefully. Thousands of them were dying as ships from Britain and other nations transported them across the Atlantic. Would Mrs. Henson's prayer for freedom from slavery ever be answered? A major part of the answer had just entered the House of Commons.

'I saw a little fellow on a
table speaking, a perfect
shrimp, but presently the
shrimp swelled into a whale.'
James Boswell
on
William Wilberforce

The Shrimp who swelled into a Whale

'I would go anywhere to hear that chap Wilberforce sing!' the Prince of Wales is said to have told the Duchess of Devonshire.

He certainly did plenty of singing. When Wilberforce became a Member of Parliament he was welcomed to the luxurious clubs and great private homes of London, not only because he was rich but because he was full of jokes and fun and because he could sing. He was the life and soul of many a party.

He went to the opera, to the theatre, and to the pleasure gardens of Vauxhall. Everywhere he went he was constantly mimicking famous politicians.

'Go on, Wilberforce, let's hear you 'do' the Prime Minister, Lord North,' his friends would urge him. Immediately William, whether he was in a coffee house near to the House of Commons or in some great mansion would begin to mimic the Prime Minister to perfection. His friends thought it was hilarious, and so it was!

Wilberforce began to learn all the necessary skills to be a good Member of Parliament. His friendship with William Pitt, who also entered the House of Commons as a Member of Parliament in January 1781, deepened.

Pitt was shy, but cool and confident while William was emotional, impulsive and excitable. Wilberforce looked on Pitt as his hero and Pitt called Wilberforce his 'good angel.' Both men were to have a huge effect on history. Within twenty months of entering the House of Commons Pitt was made the Chancellor of the Exchequer.

'A holiday, my dear Pitt, a holiday! That's what we need!' said Wilberforce enthusiastically one morning.

'And where shall we go?' asked Pitt.

'France, let's go to France,' said Wilberforce.

'Agreed,' said Pitt, and they began to make plans. Soon they crossed the English Channel and arrived in the city of Rheims. Unfortunately they had forgotten to bring proper identification papers with them and the only person to whom they had an introduction in the city was a grocer. As they walked through the city a policeman thought they looked rather suspicious and reported them to the authorities.

'No! No!' said a local priest, who found out about the situation,

'I know who these men are! This is William Pitt, the Chancellor of the Exchequer in the British House of Commons and this is William Wilberforce, the Member of Parliament for the British town of Hull. You must give them free passage!'

'They looked suspicious to me,' said the policeman.

'If you arrest them you will have the British Army coming to rescue them!' quipped the priest.

'Let's go, gentlemen!' said the priest, getting them into a carriage and taking them off to the mansion of the Archbishop of Rheims. He was delighted to meet the two British Parliamentarians and soon they were dining with him.

'Do you play billiards, gentlemen?' asked the Archbishop.

'Certainly,' replied the two Williams.

'This way, then,' said the Archbishop, leading them to the large billiard room in his mansion, '… and tell me,' he continued, 'do you know the name of Tallyrand?'

'Do you mean Tallyrand, the great diplomat?' said Pitt.

'The very one,' said the Archbishop. 'He is my nephew.'

'He is one of the most distinguished politicians in all of Europe,' said Pitt.

Soon a carriage left the city of Rheims as the two friends began their journey to Paris, with an introduction to the French Court. They arrived at the glittering Palace of Versailles, built by the King of France, Louis XIV.

'Look at it all,' said Pitt, 'No wonder his subjects call him 'The Sun King'. I have never seen extravagance like this in all of my life. Look at these furnishings and look at these decorations.'

'And as for these women,' whispered Wilberforce, 'Look at those tall headdresses. I declare, Pitt, there's a woman over there with a model of a ship on her piled up hair!'

'And there is another with ornamented birds in hers,' said Pitt laughing. 'How do they ever keep their hair stiff enough to hold these concoctions up?'

'They stick it with pomatum,' answered the knowledgeable Pitt. 'And how they ever get in and out of carriages with those hooped skirts is anybody's guess,' said Pitt.

They were then led in to meet one of the most famous Queens in history, Marie Antoinette. The fifteenth child of the Holy Roman Emperor, Francis I, who ruled over Austria, Hungary and Bohemia. Marie Antoinette was married to Louis XVI at fifteen years of age. She soon became very unpopular, both in the French Court and in France, because of her extravagance.

'I hear,' she said to Wilberforce and Pitt, 'the only person you knew in Rheims was a grocer!' She found this information very amusing, and indeed it was part of her problem. She lived in such luxury that she had no understanding of poorer conditions in which most people lived. Eventually, when the French Revolution came she and her husband were imprisoned in Paris. They later secretly escaped with their family, but were recaptured and executed in 1793.

You would never have guessed such events could have happened when Pitt and Wilberforce were at Versailles in 1783!

As it turned out the King's chief courtier

offered Pitt his daughter, Germaine, in marriage but Pitt replied with a phrase which has since gone down in history: 'Sir,' he said, 'I am already married to my country!'

Germaine became a very gifted writer, and later described Wilberforce as the wittiest, best-loved and most 'highly considered man in all England.'

Wilberforce also met the King, Louis XVI, who had the longest reign and the greatest power of all French kings. He worked very hard and took his duties as supreme ruler very seriously. He could be charming and gracious, and impressed all France, even all Europe, at that time, with gorgeous Royal ceremonies and elaborate court life. Wilberforce, though, was not very impressed with him. He later described the King in his diary as a 'clumsy, strange figure in immense boots.'

Wilberforce was also introduced at this time to Benjamin Franklin, the great American, who eventually persuaded the French to become an ally of the colonists against Britain in the American War of Independence. He also helped to draw up, and actually signed, the Declaration of Independence. Benjamin Franklin was a highly gifted man who also invented the lightning conductor!

So after meeting all these distinguished people the two friends returned to England and were soon back into their work in Parliament. Two months later Wilberforce discovered that King George III had sent for Pitt.

'I wonder what he is up to?' Wilberforce asked a friend of his. 'Wouldn't you love to know what those two are discussing at the Palace?'

'I think the King wants Pitt to be Prime Minister!' replied his friend.

'Prime Minister,' said Wilberforce with enthusiasm, 'do you really think so?'

The next day the news was out all across London and soon it was spreading all across the nation. William Pitt had become British Prime Minister at 24 years of age! This has never since been equalled.

Life, though, for Pitt was not easy because he had a lot of opposition in Parliament. A rhyme was made up by those who opposed him. It went:

'A sight to make
surrounding nations stare,
A kingdom trusted
to a schoolboy's care.'

Pitt now desperately needed and depended upon the support of Wilberforce both in and outside of

Parliament, in private and in public. He found his friend a tower of strength. The Prime Minister lived at Downing Street during the week and stayed at Wilberforce's home in Wimbledon at the weekend.

Wilberforce had inherited his house at Wimbledon on the death of his uncle. Together, they would ride horses in the countryside, have fencing matches in the garden, and talk deep into the night with their friends.

In Great Britain the life of a Parliament is normally four years and then its members have to be re-elected. When a Prime Minister declares that a Parliament's time has come to an end it is called the dissolution of Parliament. Its members then have to 'go to the country' and face a voting process that may or may not return them to the House of Commons. It is an opportunity for great discussion, argument and excitement.

This time was now approaching in England and Wilberforce decided to do something very bold. He declared that he wanted to represent the entire County of Yorkshire and not just the city of Hull in the next Parliament.

'But William, have you any idea of how

difficult a task you are setting yourself?' said Pitt when he heard of it. 'With due respect to you, my friend, the rich and aristocratic families of the County of Yorkshire will not take kindly to you. You are really up against a huge political battle and I am far from sure that you could win.'

'Oh! I know that the great families of the County don't want to place the son of a Hull merchant in so high a situation,' replied Wilberforce, 'but Yorkshire is the largest constituency in all of Britain and has the largest electorate. I can serve you, my dear Pitt, and the King much better as a Member of Parliament for the County of Yorkshire than ever I can as a Member for the town of Hull.'

'But what about your health?' asked Pitt anxiously. 'Will it hold out against the tremendous pressures of this coming political battle?'

'Where there's a will there's a way!' replied Wilberforce, 'health or no health I'm going to go for this position!'

* * * *

Imagine then, the scene at a meeting called in the yard of York Castle in Yorkshire on March 25th, 1784. It had been called to give what was known as 'A loyal address to the King', and was partly also called to give support to the Prime Minister, William Pitt.

Wilberforce knew that if he did well he could not only help his friend, but also raise his chances of becoming a parliamentary candidate for Yorkshire. The County returned two Members to Parliament and William was determined to be one of them. His future would swing on a very important speech he would make that afternoon.

The day before his speech he went for a long walk in the country, alone, and worried about what might happen.

'How will I do?' he mused. 'How will the people receive me? Will I be heckled and shouted at? Will the rich landowning voters ignore me?'

He didn't know but he was determined to try.

The following day, a Thursday, was bitterly cold and wet with hail storms. Over a thousand people, mostly landowners and wealthy traders, cut by a biting wind, listened to speakers who used a table as their platform, protected by a wooden canopy.

'This way, my Lord!' cried a voice in the

crowd. Lord John Cavendish had just arrived in a magnificent coach drawn by four horses.

Not far away stood his brother, the Duke of Devonshire, Lord Surrey and the Earls of Effingham and Faucouberg.

'This chap Wilberforce hasn't a hope of election,' said Lord John Cavendish to his brother.

'I know of his ambitions,' replied the Duke of Devonshire 'and my rule is that you don't trust a trader's son!'

For five hours speaker after speaker presented his case, and by 4 pm. the crowd began to melt away. At last, the slender Wilberforce eagerly got up on to the table and began to speak. The crowd stopped in its tracks. Who was this young fellow with a voice that reached the furthest end of the crowd? He spoke, not in great phrases, but in language everyone could understand. His words, though spoken fast, were full of warmth and wit and enthusiasm.

'Bravo! Bravo!' shouted someone, enthusiastically.

'Go for it!' urged another.

'True!' roared another supporter.

Wilberforce's speech was constantly interrupted by cheers and handclapping.

Standing in the audience was James Boswell, a famous writer of the time.

'I saw a little fellow on a table speaking,' he later recalled, 'a perfect shrimp, but presently the shrimp swelled into a whale.'

The crowd, gripped by the speaking of Wilberforce for nearly an hour, were suddenly interrupted by a King's messenger. He rode his horse into the castle yard, alighted, and began to push his way through the crowd.

'A message for you, Mr Wilberforce!' he said, out of breath, 'it is directly from the Prime Minister, Mr William Pitt!'

William paused and read the letter. The crowd watched and waited with curiosity to see his reaction. The letter announced that under the Prime Minister's authority the present Parliament had been dissolved that very day. A General Election had been declared. The messenger could not have come at a more dramatic moment.

Wilberforce announced the contents of the letter and immediately the crowd responded.

'We will have this man for our County Member,' came shouts of support, and they did.

On April 6th William Wilberforce and

a man called Duncombe were elected to represent Yorkshire in the next Parliament. It seemed to be the greatest moment in William's life so far. As it turned out, a far greater event, was about to happen, something which not only affected the destiny of slaves but was to alter the future of his soul for eternity.

'As soon as I reflected seriously upon these subjects the deep guilt and black ingratitude of my past life forced itself upon me in the strongest colours and I condemn myself for having wasted my precious time and opportunities and talents.'
William Wilberforce

Oh Happy Day

'Happy birthday, Mr. Wilberforce!' said a jockey as he passed the new Member of Parliament for Yorkshire at the York races.

'Thank you, John!' said Wilberforce, 'and see to it that we win today!'

'I'll do my best, Sir,' replied the jockey, 'your horse is running well at the moment.'

It was Wilberforce's 25th birthday and as a racehorse owner and steward at the races he was enjoying the day very much.

'Have a good holiday in France, Sir. I wish I was going with you,' said the jockey as he mounted William's racehorse.

Wilberforce had decided to take his mother and sister on a winter holiday on the French-Italian Riviera. His sister's health had not been good and he felt that he, too, needed a rest.

So, with his mother, his sister, his cousin

Bessie Smith, and his friend Isaac Milner, now a tutor at Queen's College, Cambridge, he sailed from Dover to Calais on October 20th, 1784. Wilberforce felt that Isaac Milner, who was a very knowledgeable and lively individual, would make a good companion on his holiday.

'Let's put our carriages on boats,' said Wilberforce when they arrived at the River Rhone at Lyons.

'Superb,' said Milner. 'It will beat those bumpy roads we have been on!'

They sailed down the Rhone for four days, their hours filled with witty and pleasant conversation, and eventually they reached Avignon. The weather was beautiful as they toured the Marseilles region and the Cote d'Azur. Their conversation, though, soon began to turn to matters of religion.

Wilberforce was no atheist but had not committed himself to the Lord Jesus as his personal Saviour. He had long buried the impressions he had received as a child from his uncle and aunt. Milner, on the other hand, was now an ordained Church of England Minister as well as being a tutor. He was a very devout Christian.

'I can't stand those Methodists,' said

Wilberforce one morning, as their carriage bumped along the highway. 'Their views are held only by vulgar or at least uninformed enthusiastic people. I go to hear a preacher in London called Lindsey. He does not believe that the Lord Jesus was God or that He died for our sins or that the Bible is all true.'

On and on Wilberforce would argue and ridicule what he had learned in his childhood. Lindsey's views had reached deep into his heart and soul and he had no time for those people who opposed him, particularly those known as Evangelicals.

'Now Wilberforce, I don't pretend to be a match for you in this sort of running fire of argument. But if you really wish to discuss these topics in a serious and argumentative way I will be very happy to enter on them with you.'

Milner's great gift was being able to explain complex things, simply. His explanations of the heart of the Christian Gospel, though, did not make a lot of impact on Wilberforce.

Their carriage eventually travelled towards Nice where Mrs Wilberforce had rented a house. They all had a delightful holiday going out riding each day and enjoying the brilliant Mediterranean sunshine.

One morning the postman arrived at the door.

'A letter from London,' he said, handing William quite a large package.

'Looks important,' said Milner.

'It's from the Prime Minister,' said William, setting down his cup of coffee and beginning to read, avidly.

'What does he say?' asked his sister Sarah.

'I'm afraid the letter pleads with me to return to England as soon as possible. The Prime Minister needs my help to get some reforms through Parliament.'

'Then you go where you're needed,' said his mother. 'We will stay on here for the rest of our holiday.'

The house was soon bustling with all the excitement of packing and in the midst of it William casually lifted a book which was lying on a sideboard.

'What's this?' he asked, picking up the book which belonged to his cousin Bessie. He began to leaf through it.

'It is one of the best books ever written,' replied Milner, 'Let's take it with us and read it on our journey. It's by a chap called Philip Doddridge.'

All across the world today choirs sing a very famous hymn written by Philip Doddridge. It's called, 'Oh Happy Day' and it tells of the joy and pleasure a person receives on coming to know the Lord Jesus, personally.

Doddridge's book was packed with the rest of their belongings and Milner and Wilberforce set out on their long journey to England, bumping along the rutted and ill-made roads of France.

All the way back to England the two friends discussed the things that Doddridge said in his book.

Milner spoke to William of the need for repentance from sin, for forgiveness available through the Lord Jesus, and of the fact that the Lord Jesus' blood had been shed on the cross to cleanse from all sin. Milner helped William to understand that the Gospel of Jesus Christ is the best news the world has ever heard.

'Ah Milner! I used to love those truths as a lad in my aunt and uncle's home. I used to listen to the Rev John Newton, and other famous preachers speak of them. I used to sing about them in those Methodist hymns they taught me, but I have long since left them behind. Now I find myself being challenged to believe all that you are telling me the Bible teaches.'

God was at work in William Wilberforce's mind and heart through the Holy Spirit and slowly he was being drawn to put his trust in the Lord Jesus as his Saviour.

'After all, Wilberforce, Jesus did say, "Come to Me all you who labour and are heavy laden and I will give you rest. Take My yoke upon you and learn of Me for My yoke is easy and My burden is light." You can know that rest and peace that Jesus speaks of, William,' said Milner.

As the snows began to fall across Europe and cover the passing countryside, William began to feel a deep sense of sorrow for the times he had wasted in frivolous behaviour. He began to long to know and serve God.

The weather around them began to worsen as winter truly set in, and one day at the top of a hill in Burgundy the weight of the carriage overpowered the horses. Stumbling, they started to slide helplessly towards a corner which they could not turn. On the other side lay a huge precipice. Wilberforce, who had been panting up the hill behind the carriage, saw to his horror that the carriage was rolling towards it.

Milner was walking beside the carriage

and seeing what was happening, immediately put his shoulder against the wheel and held it by his powerful strength.

'Stand clear, Milner!' shouted Wilberforce expecting his friend to fall over the edge at any moment. 'Please don't be a fool, let the carriage go.' But Milner stood his ground until the horses, now eased of the weight, were coaxed back by the young driver.

'Thank God you're safe, Milner. I really thought you were going to be dragged out over that precipice. What a crazy thing to do!' said a very frightened Wilberforce.

Eventually they arrived in England and their carriage entered Downing Street in London where Milner left Wilberforce with his friend, the Prime Minister.

Wilberforce was a changed man. In his mind he had come to agree wholeheartedly that what the Bible taught was true. That decision was to change his whole attitude to life.

* * * *

In the weeks leading to summer, Wilberforce stood by Pitt in some proposals which would give Ireland trade concessions.

The people of Yorkshire, however, felt that this would not help their woollen industry. Wilberforce was criticised, but he bravely stood by Ireland which was facing great economic distress. Although the proposals did not go through, William showed great courage in supporting them.

In late June William returned to the Continent for further travels with his family and Milner, visiting France, Italy and Switzerland.

'Let's read the New Testament together, Milner,' he said after dinner one evening in a Swiss inn. He enjoyed his studies of the Scriptures with Milner, and even as they journeyed in their carriage they continued to read and talk about the Bible. William, though, not only began to examine the New Testament but to truly examine his life and where it was heading. He wrote in his diary:

'As soon as I reflected seriously upon these subjects the deep guilt and black ingratitude of my past life forced itself upon me in the strongest colours and I condemn myself for having wasted my precious time and opportunities and talents.'

He realised that he was not yet a Christian.

When William returned to London he was in absolute despair. He could find no peace with God. He decided it would be better for him to withdraw from public life and go away by himself.

He gave up playing cards and the theatre and resigned from the five clubs he belonged to in London. Yet, despite all this, peace with God did not come.

'I will go out of my mind if I don't find some spiritual counsellor,' he said to a friend one day.

'The man you should consult is John Newton, the Rector of St Mary's Woolnoth Church in London,' said his friend. 'Why not write to him and ask him for an interview? The old African blasphemer, as they call him, should understand all about sinners like you: he's been a wicked sinner himself and that makes him different from ordinary parsons.'

William's friend went away laughing but William didn't laugh. He now remembered his boyhood hero, the Minister whose stories he listened to so eagerly in the past.

'Perhaps he won't help me,' thought William. 'My friends all despise people like the Rev Newton and evangelical Christians like him! If they find out that I am interested in these things I will have no friends left. Should I write to the man? I feel I must.'

William sent off a letter and patiently waited for a reply. It was not long in coming. Newton said he would be delighted to see him.

It was at seven o'clock on a cold winter's morning that Wilberforce set out from his apartments in The Strand. Slowly he walked along Fleet Street towards Ludgate Hill and the square mile which is known as the City of London.

John Newton's church was near the busy Wool Exchange where merchants bought and sold wool all day. Newton's house, about a mile distant from the church, was in Charles Square. William had pleaded with Newton to keep his visit a secret but now that he approached his house he hesitated.

'What shall I say to him?' he thought. 'How can I ever describe the feelings in my heart and the doubts and fears that I have about getting to know God and trying to serve Him.'

William, who had never found it difficult to talk anywhere, was now tongue-tied. He walked twice around The Square in despair and then summing up courage, he strode up the steps of Newton's house and rang the doorbell.

'It is hoped and believed that
the Lord has raised you up for
the good of his church and for
the good of the nation.'
John Newton
to
William Wilberforce

Amazing Grace

The man who greeted the troubled William Wilberforce was now sixty years of age, and his life had been filled with astonishing adventures.

John Newton's father had been a very experienced sea captain and John had had a lot of experience at sea under his father's command. He had been well trained, reaching the position of third mate by the time he was seventeen.

One evening, the seventeen year old John, who was very much in love with a girl called Polly Catlett, decided that he must ride to see her. He had been waiting to join a ship for quite some time and his father kept giving him a very serious warning.

'Be on the lookout for press gangs, lad,' he warned. 'There is a rumour running abroad that France is about to attack England in a dispute over the Austrian succession. His Majesty's ships will be looking for merchant seamen to force into the Royal Navy. If you run into them you've had it. You haven't got a Certificate of Protection until you join a new ship. If you had they could not touch you.'

'Oh, I'll be alright, father,' John kept saying. 'They'll never catch me. I'll keep a sharp eye out for them.'

On this particular evening though, John Newton's thoughts were not on press gangs, but upon Polly. She lived at Aveley in Kent, not very far from the naval yards at Chatham on the Thames Estuary. Press gangs were indeed very busy and John rode right into one that evening.

'Halt,' cried a naval Lieutenant in uniform. Around him stood a group of scarlet-coated soldiers with their rifles fixed on John. He immediately reined in his horse.

'Where are you going?'

'To see my girlfriend at Aveley,' said John.

'Get down,' said the Lieutenant, gruffly.

'You're a sailor, I can see it by the way you walk,' said the Officer as John walked towards him.

'I am indeed, Sir, I am a Merchant Seaman and have served as a third mate.'

'You're going to serve in the Royal Navy now,' said the Lieutenant smiling.

'But I have served as an officer and should not be taken into the Navy as a common seaman,' pleaded John.

It was no use. John was put under guard in the back room of an inn while the press gang went to look for more seamen.

He was allowed, though, to scribble a note to his father.

'Here, lad,' said John calling to a boy he saw through the open door, 'Take this note to this address. It is a note to my father. Here is some money for your trouble.'

'Do you want it taken in a hurry, Sir,' said the lad.

'Run for your life, lad, and don't stop until you find him,' urged John.

Soon the little back room of the inn was filled with nine other men who had been press ganged.

'Tis a terrible thing they do,' said one, 'what are my wife and children going to think?'

'I have a very sick mother,' said another, 'she desperately needs me. This whole thing is not fair.'

Suddenly, in the outer inn, John heard raised voices.

'Where is he, where is he?' said a voice that was very familiar. It was his father.

'We have him under guard,' he heard the Lieutenant say sharply.

The voices continued in conversation for a long time as Captain Newton pleaded for his son.

'No, Captain Newton, I simply cannot allow him to be freed,' continued the Lieutenant. 'The French are already at sea and shots have been exchanged. They have even tried to land a force here in Kent headed by the Young Pretender, Bonny Prince Charlie. There is no way that I can release your son who has been so excellently trained by you. His Majesty's Navy needs him, desperately.'

'Let's march!' came the order and John and the other nine men were taken to the quayside. They were immediately brought down the river in a little ship called *The Betsey* and put on board *HMS Harwich*, a fifty gun man-of-war. It was Sunday, March 4th, 1744.

John Newton found himself in the company of three hundred men in the very confined space of one of the Royal Navy's smaller fighting ships.

The crew were made up of convicted criminals sentenced to naval service, other young men who had fallen foul of their parents and masters, and who had been handed over to the Navy. Dozens more had been seized by the press gangs.

Throughout the coming year *The Harwich* escorted convoys to Scotland and Norway and actually saw action in capturing a French ship off the Yorkshire coast. Eventually, after meeting a violent gale off the Cornish coast, *The Harwich* had to put in to Plymouth Sound for repairs. The captain of *The Harwich* Captain Carteret called John Newton to his cabin.

'Would you take the long boat party to fetch vegetables, fresh water and other supplies, Mr Newton,' he said, 'they are waiting on the quay at Plymouth and I solemnly remind you to take the utmost care that no man tries to desert.'

As it turned out it was John Newton who deserted. As soon as the long boat was made fast and the men's attention was taken up with loading on the supplies, John slipped away. He slept rough that evening and managed to walk twenty-five miles before he walked straight into a party of Marines searching for deserters.

'Halt!' came the dreaded word from yet

another Lieutenant, 'where are you going?'

'I have deserted my ship,' said John Newton with a crestfallen look.

He was tired and travel-stained and knew that having neither horse nor carriage nor written orders from his captain, his chances of bluffing his way through were impossible. He was marched back to Plymouth and to *The Harwich*.

Before the entire ship's company, he was stripped, tied to a wooden bench and given at least twenty-five hard strokes on his bare back with a nine-tailed whip of knotted ropes. Lashes were given slowly with a roll of drums between each one of them. The second part of his punishment was to be ordered back on duty at the earliest possible moment, despite the fact that his back had two hundred weals looking very sore and angry. He was demoted to the lowest rank of ordinary seaman. The ship then sailed from Plymouth for the East Indies on a five year voyage.

Eventually John Newton was exchanged for another seaman on board a slave ship called *The Pegasus*. It seems hard for us now to understand that the slave trade was looked upon as an acceptable trade in those days. In a year alone, one hundred and eighty-five ships were to take forty-three thousand, seven hundred and fifty-five slaves from Africa to America. Even in England it was a respectable thing to be the Captain of a slave ship.

John Newton noticed a red-faced man on board *The Pegasus*. Amos Clow, who was returning to Africa from England, wore very rich clothes and had large gold buckles on his shoes. He was one of the wealthiest slave traders on the African coast and a part-owner of *The Pegasus*.

'Mr Clow, Sir,' John asked him one day, 'I wish you would let me work for you. I have had lots of experience as a seaman and I can handle money matters. I will work harder than I have ever worked in my life.'

'I'll see what I can do,' answered Clow.

He did, and John Newton entered the service of the slave trader on what was known as Africa's Coral Coast. It was to be a disaster for him.

Clow lived with a very cruel woman on a tiny island set in the Gulf of Guinea. His mistress was an African Princess, and from the start she used every opportunity to do John Newton harm.

Whenever Clow was away on slave business the Princess half starved Newton.

Once he took a dreadful fever and lay for days on a rush mat spread on a hard wooden chest with a log of wood for his pillow. He had a raging thirst. The Princess ignored him, and then as the fever turned she had her own silver plate sent over to him. All that was left on it were the bones from her chicken and the last bits of rice which she couldn't eat herself.

As John Newton struggled to walk the next day, the Princess gave a cruel order:

'Come here,' she said to a group of her slaves. 'Do you see the way that Newton is walking? I want you to fall into step behind him and imitate everything he does. If he stumbles, you stumble, if he gropes blindly for the wall to lean upon, you do the same.'

It was a pathetic sight to see the nineteen year old, reduced to such a condition. He was so driven by hunger, he crept out of his hut to dig up the roots of young lime trees and chew their bitter, tough stalks.

'She is treating me like a virtual slave,' Newton complained bitterly to Clow in the Princess' presence. 'I almost died of starvation while you were gone and all she did most of the time was mock me.'

Sadly for Newton, Clow didn't believe a word that he said.

In fact things got a lot worse for him and when slave ships bound for England stopped at the islands the sailors on board used to point at him and laugh. They had never seen an English slave before.

John Newton knew that he would have to do something to escape from the awful condition of slavery he had fallen into.

'Could you smuggle me some writing materials from one of those ships that call in the bay?' he asked Clow's house slave one day.

The slave had proved to be very friendly, and had occasionally risked the anger of Clow by bringing John some leftovers to eat from his master's table.

'I'll try,' he said, 'but if my master catches me I will be in big trouble.'

Eventually the slave managed to smuggle some writing materials to John and he wrote a letter to his father.

'How on earth can I ever get this to my father?' John asked the slave.

'I'll put it secretly into Clow's bag before it is sealed to be taken on board. The bag contains all sorts of documents directed to his trade.'

After many months John's letter reached home and his father asked a friend of his, Captain Manesty to look out for his son when doing business on the Coral Coast.

Captain Manesty eventually rescued John and he set out on board his ship, *The Greyhound* for the 7000 mile journey home to England.

The Greyhound was a small ship and had to choose her route very carefully. She carried a cargo of gold, ivory and beeswax. Her light load was to prove her salvation in the adventure that lay ahead.

For years, John Newton had been one of the most ungodly young people you could have ever come across. He lived an immoral life and tried to convert others to his atheism.

Then, an amazing experience overwhelmed him. *The Greyhound* ran into a huge storm off the coast of Newfoundland. For days on end the ship tossed like a bottle in mountainous seas. Huge waves of icy water crashed through her and wrecked the upper timbers on one side. The winds blew the sails into shreds and the vessel became a virtual wreck in a very few minutes. One of the crew was swept overboard to his death leaving only twelve men to work on board. Amazingly, because of her light cargo, *The Greyhound* stayed afloat.

The storm raged on and the ship leaked dreadfully as she plunged into each valley of water. John Newton feared she would not rise again, and that they would all sink to the bottom without a trace. He was staring death in the face.

As he went to relieve a seaman at the ship's pumps Newton said to the captain, 'If this won't do, then the Lord have mercy on us!' Suddenly, John thought, 'Why should the Lord have mercy on me?'

Looking out into that awful sea he began to think about the Lord Jesus whom He had mocked and scorned but who had died for him at Calvary.

'The more I looked at what Jesus had done at the cross, the more He met my case exactly,' he wrote later. 'I needed someone or something to stand between a righteous God and my sinful self: between a God who must punish sins and blasphemers, and myself who had wallowed in both to the neck. I needed an almighty Saviour who would step in and take my sins away.'

He found that Saviour in the Lord Jesus Christ and repenting of his sins he became a Christian right there in those mountainous seas off the North Atlantic.

Twenty-seven days after the storm had

first hit *The Greyhound* a lookout cried, 'Land Ahoy!'

On 8th April 1748 the ship rounded Dunree Head on the Donegal coast in Ireland and limped up Lough Swilly, anchoring beneath Buncrana Castle.

John Newton had many adventures following his conversion and, like millions around him still did not question whether the slave trade was morally right. It had flourished for centuries and he saw no problem in being part of it. Eventually he became a slave-ship's captain and commanded two ships, *The Duke of Argyle* and *The African*, making long voyages to the Gulf of Guinea and the Americas.

After his marriage to Polly Catlett, the girl he loved from childhood, John Newton began to grow tired of the long separations from his wife.

'Polly,' he said one day, 'I am really beginning to loathe being a Captain in the slave trade. I hate being constantly involved with chains, bolts and shackles. I dislike being a jailer to the slaves I am carrying and I am praying to God for a better way of life.'

Amazingly, through the influence of the great preachers, George Whitfield, John Wesley and others, John Newton eventually became a Christian minister in the Church of England. He remained in ministry for forty-three years and became one of the most powerful influences for God in his nation.

The children were fascinated by Newton's sea stories and sense of humour. No child had loved him more than the young William Wilberforce who used to listen to the amazing ex-sea captain and slaver when he preached in London. He once wrote that he 'reverenced him as a parent when I was a child.'

It was of course John Newton who wrote one of the greatest hymns of the Christian faith. It is called 'Amazing Grace' and describes how God's grace and kindness found him and saved him. The words are very moving:

Amazing Grace! How sweet the sound
That saved a wretch like me,
I once was lost, but now am found,
Was blind but now I see.

'Twas grace that taught my heart to fear,
And grace my fears relieved.
How precious did that grace appear
The hour I first believed.

Through many dangers, toils and snares
I have already come;
'Tis grace has brought me safe this far
And grace will lead me home.

When we've been there ten thousand years
Bright shining as the sun,
We've no less days to sing God's praise
Than when we first begun.

Now that very same John Newton stood on the steps of the Rectory, holding out his hand enthusiastically to welcome the brilliant Member of Parliament for Yorkshire.

Little did either know that their meeting was to change history.

'It is a business, William, at
which my heart now shudders.
God forgive me that I ever
took part in it.'
John Newton
on the slave trade

The Truth about the Slave Trade

'Good morning Mr Wilberforce!' said the Rev Newton, 'I can tell you it is not often that I have a Member of Parliament calling with me.'

'It's very good of you to see me, Mr Newton,' said William, still feeling very nervous.

'What is your problem?' said the minister trying to make his depressed and unhappy caller feel more comfortable.

'I want to follow the Lord Jesus,' said Wilberforce, 'but I don't think I can be a good Christian and a Member of Parliament. I love my political work but surely that is not suitable for a Christian. Surely it is better that I serve God in a world far removed from politics. There are so many men in parliament who do not believe the Christian Gospel.'

We do not know the full answer that John Newton gave to Wilberforce's questions but what we do know is that he was used by God to encourage Wilberforce to see that he could be mightily used by God as a Member of Parliament. He urged him to stay in Parliament and to be an influence for good. This, of course, is what the Bible teaches all Christians should be in whatever job God calls them to do. The Bible is full of stories of people who lived for the Lord where plenty of unbelievers worked.

Joseph, for example, was Governor of Egypt under a Pharaoh who did not know the Lord and Daniel served as a very powerful leader in the governments of quite a few godless kings in his generation.

The Lord Jesus said in Matthew chapter 9 and verse 12:

"Those who are well have no need of a doctor, but only those who are sick".

What Jesus was saying was that if a doctor spent his whole life among people who were well he would never be able to do any good for those who were ill. He was asking those who followed Him to be good witnesses for Him among those who desperately needed to hear the good news of his Gospel.

If Christians just stayed among Christians then they would never get Christ's good news to those who need it most.

As William Wilberforce left John Newton's home that morning in December and headed back to his apartments in The Strand, he was a much quieter and calmer person. He now knew that to follow Christ did not mean he had to leave Parliament. Somehow he began to feel that God had a purpose for his life. He no longer needed to have the awful feeling and knowledge that he was wasting his time and talent. At Easter 1786 Wilberforce went to spend time with a friend of his called William Unwin, the rector of Stock in Essex. The Rev Unwin was used by God to help draw William back to those wonderful truths he had believed in childhood and to a settled faith in Jesus Christ as his Saviour and Lord.

Soon after sunrise on Easter morning William went out into the fields to pray. He later wrote to his sister Sally describing how he gave thanks on that morning. 'Amid that general chorus with which all nature seems on such a morning to be swelling the song of praise and thanksgiving.'

* * * *

William now began to have a deep friendship with the ex-slave trader, the Rev John Newton who began to tell of his adventures and the frightening conditions of slavery which he had witnessed.

'It is a business, William, at which my heart now shudders,' he said one day, 'God forgive me that I ever took part in it.'

We do not know when William first became deeply interested in doing something about the slave trade but one thing is certain that in October 1786 he received a letter from a friend, Sir Charles Middleton urging him to raise the question of the slave trade in Parliament.

Sir Charles Middleton was a Member of Parliament himself and a very keen Christian. He and his wife believed that Wilberforce was just the man to take up the cause for the abolition of slavery and to champion the cause in Parliament.

Wilberforce replied that he felt very unequal to the task but promised that he would not 'positively decline it.' He agreed to go and see Lord and Lady Middleton and hold discussions with them.

One fine morning his carriage rolled up to the Middleton's home at Barham Court, near Maidstone in Kent.

'Good morning Mr. Wilberforce, it is so good of you to come to see us. Come right in,' said Sir Charles.

When they eventually settled in the large drawing room Lord and Lady Middleton pleaded with Wilberforce to fight against slavery.

'But I don't know a lot about it,' said Wilberforce.

'We know people who have the facts in detail,' said Sir Charle. 'All that is necessary is that you decide to give yourself to it. We will back you with all the help we can.'

When William returned to his newly leased house at 4 Old Palace Yard, opposite the entrance to the House of Lords, he was a new man.

A conviction had begun to rise in his heart that he might indeed be the very man that God wanted to lead this great campaign. Early in 1787 he received a young clergyman called Thomas Clarkson who had written a very famous essay on slavery which was beginning to stir people all over the nation.

'I am utterly convinced that you are the man, Mr Wilberforce, to move for abolition in the House of Commons and I have many other friends who feel the same,' Clarkson told him.

So it was that one beautiful evening in May 1787 that Wilberforce called to see his friend the Prime Minister at his new country house at Hallwood in Kent. They went out into the garden and sat under an oak tree to have a talk. It was there as the shadows lengthened across the lawn at Hallwood House, that the Prime Minister convinced William Wilberforce that he was the man to abolish slavery.

'Why don't you give notice of a Motion on the subject of the slave trade and I will support you in the British House of Commons?' said Pitt.

The system by which an Act of Parliament is passed in the British House of Commons is quite complicated.

First of all the Member of Parliament has to ask permission to bring a Bill before the House. If the House agrees to this first move, called a Motion or a Resolution, the Bill is written up, printed and circulated among Members. This is the First Reading of a Bill. It is then discussed at a Second Reading and, if passed, is then examined and amended by a Committee of Members who are specially interested in it. It must then be discussed at a Third Reading and, if passed, it goes to the House of Lords who also read it three times.

If the Bill is passed by both Houses it then receives the King or Queen's assent and becomes an Act of Parliament.

'I know that it will be a very difficult task for you, William,' said the Prime Minister, 'for all the sugar on all the tables of England and all the rum in the British Navy comes from the West Indies where the plantations are worked by slaves. People will argue that if you end the slave trade it will make this nation economically poor.'

Many people make a lot of money through this trade, William, and they will not be happy if you stop money flowing to them.'

'I know that what you are saying is true,' answered Wilberforce, 'but I am not afraid to undertake it, now. I am convinced that the Lord is leading me to this work and I am prepared to work at it and go on until the wicked trade is wiped off the face of the earth.'

The slave trade has been on earth for a very long time. It is a shameful fact that, even today, slavery is still a problem in many countries. Sadly, it has been an accepted part of all ancient civilisation, including those in the Middle East, China and India.

William Wilberforce discovered that in 1562, John Hawkins, an English seaman in the time of Queen Elizabeth I, kidnapped three hundred Africans in Sierra Leone and sold them to the Spanish planters of San Domingo.

Following that a company called the African Company was formed to supply African slaves to the West Indies and to the Southern State of North America. The climate was too hot in these regions for white settlers to work the cotton, tobacco, sugar and rice plantations. Africans were very strong physically and had been used to a lot of heat. Slaves were therefore in great demand and those who supplied them to the plantation owners made a lot of money.

Even England, when she made peace with France and Spain after a long war in 1713, insisted that she be allowed the right to supply slaves to the Spanish colonies.

In the early months of 1787 Thomas Clarkson called each week at Palace Yard to give Wilberforce evidence and information about the slave trade.

'How many slaves do you think are being shipped across the Atlantic in a year from Africa, Thomas?' asked William one morning.

'One hundred thousand, Mr. Wilberforce at least.'

'And how many of these slaves are carried in British ships?'

'More than half', answered Clarkson.

'Tell me the detail of the routes that these ships take?' asked Wilberforce, obviously stunned by the depth to which Britain was involved in this awful practice.

'The normal pattern,' answered Clarkson, 'is that ships leave Liverpool, London and Bristol with textiles, beads and bangles, brandy and gunpowder and other articles that appeal to Africans. It takes them about five or six weeks to sail to the West African coast.'

'And how do the Africans feel when they see the slave ships coming?' asked Wilberforce.

'Frightened out of their minds,' answered Clarkson. 'The season of the slave ships is a time of terror and violence. There are at least three methods used to obtain slaves. They are either seized by armed kidnap, bought from professional traders who have captured them in the African interior and brought them to the coast for sale, or they are bartered for by slave captains with local chiefs. These chiefs will actually order their soldiers to round up a neighbouring village at night and bring back all their captives.

'Sometimes chiefs will go to war with other chiefs and tribes with other tribes. Defeat means slavery, victory means huge wealth.'

'That is terrible,' said Wilberforce, visibly moved by what he had heard.

He joined the Society for the Abolition of the Slave Trade and listened with growing horror to the tales that Thomas Clarkson would tell of trips he had made to Liverpool and Bristol to find out what was going on. Clarkson boarded slave ships and asked a lot of questions around the docklands.

He brought back shackles, handcuffs, mouth-openers and thumbscrews, all instruments of torture used upon slaves. He also brought with him, branding irons used for burning the initial of the owners on the shoulders of their slaves, and large iron neck collars which stopped slaves from escaping.

'Tell me, Clarkson,' asked Wilberforce, 'who are we up against in this campaign? What groups of people are likely to oppose us?'

Clarkson sighed, 'The slave agents, the plantation owners in the English colonies, naval captains and officers, wealthy aristocrats who build large mansions with the money they make in the plantations they own. You can also expect opposition from officials of state in Britain who back this whole system up.'

Looking at Wilberforce he added, 'All of these people form a very powerful influence that keeps the slave trade in place.'

'Yes, you are right Clarkson, and the vast majority of people in England couldn't care less about the sufferings of these people thousands of miles away,' said Wilberforce sadly.

'But we do,' answered Clarkson, 'and with the help of God and our friends across the nation we will put a stop to this dreadful trade.'

One thing is for certain, they had a very tough job on their hands.

'Almighty God, under all my weakness and uncertain prospects give me grace to trust firmly in Thee, that I may not sink under my sorrows nor be disquieted with the fears of those evils which cannot without Thy permission fall upon me.'
William Wilberforce

Mr Greatheart

'There are too many people being hanged in England,' said Wilberforce to his friend Bishop Porteous.

'I agree, William,' said the Bishop.

'Well, let's do something about it,' said Wilberforce.

'There's not a lot we can do about the hangings, William,' said a doubtful Bishop.

'Oh yes there is,' said William, 'if we can reform the behaviour of people in England then we can empty the prisons and cheat the gallows.'

It was a very brave Wilberforce who early in 1787, while in the middle of his deep involvement in the abolition of the slave trade, set out to do something about the frightening behaviour of people all across Georgian England.

'Look at the state of the country!' said Wilberforce in frustration, 'drunkenness, immorality, bad language, gambling, treating God's Name lightly, ignoring God's commandments, cruelty to animals, cruelty to children, immoral books and pictures, the whole country is flooded with it all.'

'But what is your plan, William?' asked Bishop Porteous.

'I am going to get the King to reissue his proclamation for the encouragement of devotion to God and good behaviour,' said Wilberforce.

And that is exactly what he did! On June 1st, 1787 George III reissued his proclamation. All across the nation, as people read their newspapers, they had no idea that the influence behind what they were reading was a 27 year old Member of Parliament for Yorkshire.

The proclamation called for a return to public worship in churches on Sundays, and for judges, sheriffs and justices to be very vigilant and strict in the discovery and punishment of people for 'excessive drinking, blasphemy, profane swearing and cursing... or other dissolute, immoral or disorderly practices.'

'I went in a coach to Whitehall and had a

dish of tea and a bit of bread and butter at The Duke of Montague's,' wrote the Earl of Ailesbury in his diary. He also added that he had found Wilberforce with the Duke, who was asking William 'to be President of a Society for carrying into execution the proclamation.'

This was the second part of Wilberforce's plan. In the summer of 1787 he travelled by carriage far and wide, calling in at the homes of the great and influential people of England to recruit membership and support for his new Proclamation Society which would assist in carrying the King's Proclamation on good behaviour into effect.

'What, Wilberforce?' laughed the Earl Fitzwilliam in Wilberforce's face, 'reform behaviour? I agree there is a lot of godless and immoral behaviour in the nation but the only way you'll ever stop it is to take away people's money. If they don't have it, then they can't buy alcohol or spend their money on vice and gambling. Ruin their wallets, man, and you'll have it! England is too wealthy for your Society to have any effect. I know you are sincere, William, but you haven't a hope.'

Wilberforce, though, refused to be stopped and if you now stand before his statue outside his birthplace in Hull you will read a very moving statement. It reads, 'The world owes him the abolition of slavery and England owes him the reformation of manners.'

Manners was a word used in Georgian times for behaviour. Earl Fitzwilliam was wrong for it is a fact that Christians, young people and men and women can influence their nation for good by standing up for what is right.

Even the practice of family prayers still practised in many homes today comes chiefly from the influence of William Wilberforce who first started it in his!

The reformation of manners in the nation was on its way despite much opposition, but the campaign against slavery was now gaining momentum. Wilberforce was frantically busy.

'Please, William, get out into the country air,' pleaded Pitt when he saw his friend in March 1788 exhausted from fever, loss of appetite and lack of sleep.

Wilberforce suffered from ill health nearly all his life. He had weak and painful eyes and a physical condition called ulcerative colitis brought on by stress.

'I can't stop working,' pleaded Wilberforce.

'If you don't stop work then it will stop you,' warned a very concerned Prime Minister.

'That little fellow cannot possibly survive twelve months,' said Dr. Richard Warren who had been called in to treat Wilberforce.

'He hasn't the stamina to last a fortnight,' said a group of doctors who looked into Wilberforce's condition.

Many felt Wilberforce was dying, but God had other plans for him and much good work for him still to accomplish. He survived to face the greatest battle of his life.

For example, his friend Sir William Young who owned 1300 slaves and three islands would by no means be pleased if his slaves were freed.

Wilberforce knew that he might even be attacked physically by mobs or individuals. One of his prayers is on record at this time:

'Almighty God,' he prayed, 'under all my weakness and uncertain prospects give me grace to trust firmly in Thee, that I may not sink under my sorrows nor be disquieted with the fears of those evils which cannot without Thy permission fall upon me.'

The 12th May 1789 turned out to be one of the most important days in the life of William Wilberforce.

For months he had been preparing for this day, writing pamphlets on the slave trade and articles on slavery for the newspapers. He had spoken passionately at public meetings, using the statue of a slave in chains to illustrate the cruelty of the trade.

'Look at this question very carefully,' he would declare, 'this is how Christians are treating their fellow human beings in Africa. The thing is an absolute disgrace.'

A friend of his, the English poet, William Cowper, put the whole question of the English attitude to the slave trade in a poem withering with sarcasm and power.

I own I am shocked at the purchase of slaves,
I fear those who buy them and sell them as knaves;
But I fear for their hardships, their tortures and groans,
Is almost enough to draw pity from stones.

I pity them greatly but I must be mum (quiet),
For how can we do without sugar and rum?
Especially sugar, so needful we see?
What, give up our desserts, our coffee and tea!

Besides, if we do, the French, Dutch and Danes
Will heartily thank us, no doubt, for our pains;
If we do not buy the poor creatures, they will,
And tortures and groans will be multiplied still.

If foreigners likewise would give up the trade,
Much more on behalf of your wish might be said,
But while they get riches by purchasing blacks,
Pray, tell me, why we may not also go snacks
(shares).

At 5 pm. on May 12th Wilberforce rose from his seat in the House of Commons to introduce for the first time his Bill against the slave trade. He was, in fact, feeling unwell and, at the beginning spoke slowly and quietly.

'I mean not,' he said, 'to accuse anyone but to take the shame upon myself in common with the whole Parliament ... for having suffered this horrid trade to be carried on under our authority. We are all guilty. Does the King of Bessarabia want brandy? He has only to send troops in the night to burn and desolate a village. The captives will serve as commodities that may be bartered with British traders.'

For three and a half hours the man poured out his views on the slave trade and described the true facts regarding the suffering which slaves endured, particularly in the horrendous 'Middle Passage' from Africa to the West. He told Members of Parliament that it was the facts about the Middle Passage which had driven him to take up the subject. He pleaded that slave traders and owners had no sympathy for the slaves they took.

'It is sympathy and nothing else than sympathy which is the true spring of humanity. God has commanded man, 'You shall not murder', yet the slave trade means the murder of thousands of Africans each year and is therefore contrary to the principles of justice and the laws of God.'

As Wilberforce laid out with persuasive eloquence and a wealth of detail the disgraceful facts regarding the slave trade, he suddenly turned to Irish history to back up his argument.

'Ireland used to derive a considerable trade in slaves with this country. But a great plague having infested the country, the Irish were struck with panic, suspecting that it was punishment sent from Heaven for the sin of the slave trade, and therefore abolished it. All I ask of the people of Bristol, is that they should become as civilised as the Irishmen were four hundred years ago. Let us put an end at once to this inhuman traffic.'

When eventually, exhausted, he took his seat, one of the greatest orators in England, Edmund Burke, rose to pay tribute to him.

'The House, the nation, and all Europe are under very great and serious obligation to the Honourable Gentleman, for having brought the subject forward in a manner the most masterly, impressive and eloquent. Principles so admirable, laid down with so much order and force, are equal to anything I have ever heard.'

Sadly, though, Members of Parliament decided to put off their decision on Wilberforce's Bill until the next session of Parliament. He was soon to find out there were many more disappointments on the way. Yet, deep in his heart, he was determined to carry on.

From the West Indies, though, there came a very serious setback to his campaign. A huge rebellion of slaves against their owners took place. On the island of Santo Domingo, alone, one thousand plantations were destroyed and two thousand white people were massacred. The fierceness of this rising sent waves of fear through Parliament.

'There you are, William,' his friends would say, 'how can you possibly free people like that? It would lead to a revolution similar to that which has just happened in France where the King and Queen have had their heads cut off!'

People began to turn against Wilberforce's drive to abolish the slave trade. In the middle of all this opposition a letter arrived one day for Wilberforce from the great Methodist leader, John Wesley, one week before he died. The letter was full of encouragement.

Again, Wilberforce poured out his opposition to the system under which, he said, a Captain Kimber had recently beaten a fifteen year old slave girl to death. The Prime Minister gave a great speech backing his friend. The House of Commons voted that the slave trade should cease on January 1st, 1796 but when the Bill went to the House of Lords it was defeated. The Lords said they would conduct their own enquiry into the slave trade.

Wilberforce was very deeply hurt, yet, though he did not realise it, he had slowly come to be recognised as the greatest moral leader of his country. At the prime of his life he was actually involved in 69 good causes.

'Look at those children,' he would say as he sought to help the cause of children who worked in the great spinning mills of Britain.

'Many of them are under the age of nine and enter the mill gates at five or six o'clock in the morning and do not leave until seven or eight o'clock at night. The overseers who keep an eye on them are downright wicked. They are armed with leather straps with which they punish those who are careless or who seem lazy. I know of children who have to walk a distance of twenty miles in the mill following a spinning machine during a fourteen hour day. These children also work all day Saturday, too. I think that theirs is as a great a slavery as any in the West Indies.'

Wilberforce argued in Parliament that there would be no peace or prosperity in the nations until all children were educated. He helped to establish Sunday Schools and orphanages for poor children. He helped found 'The Society for the Prevention of Cruelty to Animals', 'The Church Missionary Society', and 'The British and Foreign Bible Society' which was responsible for distributing two and a half million Bibles and New Testaments in its first fifteen years. He helped to oppose the fearful practice of using 'chimney boys' to sweep the chimneys of big houses by which many boys were choked to death by soot. He also gave away one fourth of his annual income to the poor.

One of the causes dear to Wilberforce's heart was the Sierra Leone project. A new African colony had been established with Freetown as its capital to provide a home for freed slaves. It proved to be a great success.

The truth was that William Wilberforce was becoming a very effective Christian light in an era of great spiritual darkness. He lived in a century that outwardly had great elegance and civilisation but also had a huge amount of squalor and sin.

Vast numbers of London's teenagers, for example, were involved in prostitution. Drunkenness was accepted as part of the whole social scene of the nation. Though there was huge spiritual darkness in his nation, the darker the situation, the brighter William's light shone. He was slowly becoming his nation's conscience.

'God has commanded man,
"You shall not murder", yet
the slave trade means the
murder of thousands of
Africans each year and is
therefore contrary to the
principles of justice and the
laws of God.'
William Wilberforce

The Duel

'Get out of it you miserable man!' roared a woman in the crowd that had surrounded George III's carriage.

'It's bread we need, not water,' shouted another.

'While you sit there in your posh robes and crown we sit at home starving,' cried the determined looking leader of the mob, as the King drove to open the new session of Parliament.

'Go on, open your Parliament, a fat lot of use the whole lot of you are,' screamed a woman who, with the rest of the population of London had been facing problems feeding her family.

A series of bad harvests in the country had led to a shortage of bread, and parts of England were approaching famine. The King was received with much pomp and circumstance at the House of Commons and was very glad to get out of his carriage and away from the ugly crowd.

'Let's wreck his miserable carriage,' shouted the mob leader.

They surged forward in anger and fury, and tipped over the beautiful state coach, destroying it and terrifying the poor waiting horses. England was in a very serious situation.

The French Revolution had erupted, their King and Queen had been beheaded. Raising a huge army, the French had declared themselves at war 'against all Kings and on behalf of all people.'

Wilberforce had begged the Prime Minister to lead the country clear of it, but when France declared war on Britain, the country had no choice but to fight. Wilberforce eventually spoke out particularly against the war, and Pitt and he found themselves in public opposition for the first time in their lives. Even the King was angry with Wilberforce when he heard of his speech in favour of peace. A lot of other people, including some of his constituents in Yorkshire were very discourteous to him.

Wilberforce showed great Christian kindness to the Prime Minister, despite the disagreement with him. When he heard that he was unwell he called to see him. They both realised that their friendship was far too precious and important to be broken up by their difference of opinion and soon they were back on old terms.

In Britain, the situation looked bleak. Leaflets on 'King-killing' were circulating in the streets and a man called Paine had written a book called, *The Age of Reason* which set out to undermine the Christian faith. An anti-monarchy group of people were rising in influence and crowds in the streets were now shouting for the Prime Minister to bring peace with France.

'Lob it through the front window, Dave, go on, he deserves it!' a mob leader urged. A crowd then began to stone the Prime Minister's house at No. 10 Downing Street.

'Take that Prime Minister and let the air into your brains. Give us peace and stop this war!' shouted a protestor as he continued to throw stones at more windows.

'Are they going to kill me?' wondered William Pitt who was working at No. 10 at the time of the mob's attack.

The situation was so serious that Pitt decided to bring a Seditious Meetings Bill before Parliament which would make it against the law to hold any political meetings.

Wilberforce backed him up saying it was 'a temporary sacrifice of our freedom by which the blessings of liberty may be transmitted to our children.'

One Sunday morning in 1795 Wilberforce was stepping into his carriage at Palace Yard to drive to church when he was hailed by a rider.

'Mr Wilberforce! Mr Wilberforce!' shouted the messenger as he rode up to Wilberforce's carriage, 'I have been riding through the night from Yorkshire and I have an urgent letter for you. It comes from two of your supporters.'

The letter demanded that Wilberforce come immediately to York where a huge meeting was to be held to protest at Pitt's new Bill stopping political meetings. He must come and explain why he had supported the Prime Minister.

Wilberforce went to church and then he walked round to Downing Street.

'You must go William, as quickly as you can,' said the Prime Minister, who knew all about the coming meeting of protest, 'Take my carriage and my four horses and I'll send outriders with you to clear the way.'

'What? If they find out that you've got the Prime Minister's carriage and horses they'll kill you,' joked a Member of Parliament who was also present.

'Indeed they might just do that,' said Wilberforce knowing very well that the country was in an ugly mood. With his secretary, Wilberforce headed at full speed up the Great North Road.

By night he had reached Alconbury near Huntingdon and had covered 67 miles. He had an early rise and had got beyond Doncaster after a 106 mile journey.

The next morning as William approached York, he discovered that the roads were packed with people going to the protest meeting.

'Clear the road! Clear the road!' shouted the outriders, 'Make way for the Member for Yorkshire.'

'He'll have a rough reception!' taunted a horseman as the carriage raced by.

'He might even lose his position as Member of Parliament by the time we're through with him!'

At 11 o'clock Wilberforce entered York and found his main opponent, a man called Christopher Wyvill had gathered a large meeting in the Guildhall.

'Why, it's little Wilberforce!' shouted

some in the crowd as they saw their Member of Parliament pushing his way toward the Guildhall.

'What a plucky man to come and face his opponents,' said one of Wilberforce's supporters.

Brave he certainly was but his opponent was not. He refused to come out and face the serious debate in the Castle Yard.

It was a strange situation; Wyvill had called the meeting to defend the right of everybody to say what they wanted, and now he refused to engage in a debate about free speech!

Wilberforce, with great courage, went out to address a crowd of around 4000 people. Mounting the old stone steps of the Castle Yard, he went on to speak brilliantly. The 'nightingale's' voice flowed once more and a hush fell on the crowd. He won them to his point of view, and then encouraged them to pass a petition of loyalty to the King and in favour of the Seditious Meetings Act. He won by a huge majority of votes.

The Prime Minister was also pleased when Wilberforce arrived back in London and rose in the House of Commons to prove that Christopher Wyvill's views were not representative of the majority of people in York. Wilberforce became popular again, and even the King warmed to him once more.

The King, though, was not the only one to be on friendly terms with Wilberforce!

'I'll never marry,' Wilberforce used to tell his friends. 'It's because of my ill-health and because I lead such a hectic life as a Member of Parliament. I have no time for a wife and family. After all, the French might invade England and what would that do for my married life?'

One sight of a young woman, Barbara Ann Spooner in 1796, though, was enough to change his mind. Wilberforce had been visiting Bath and Barbara, the daughter of an elderly merchant iron master, had written him a letter asking him for some spiritual advice. At their first meeting Wilberforce fell in love, and this was to deepen as the days passed. Soon he found he could not sleep for thoughts of Barbara.

'Dear Lord,' he prayed one Sunday morning, 'please guide me as to whether I should ask Barbara to marry me. I truly love her, but should I marry her?'

That morning, after church, Wilberforce and Barbara went to the famous Pump Room in Bath and as they spent time talking together Wilberforce decided to ask Barbara to marry him that very night.

He went back to his lodgings and wrote her a letter, his heart pounding with excitement and his mind filled with anxiety as to whether or not she would accept.

He need not have worried. That very night he received her reply telling him that, of course, she would marry him; poor Wilberforce couldn't sleep for happiness! It had only been seven days since he had first met her!

* * * *

'So that's the man who is trying to free the slaves!' said an onlooker in the crowd that had turned out to watch Wilberforce's wedding. It was Tuesday, May 30th 1797, and they were standing outside the Parish Church of Walnot in Bath.

'Small man, isn't he?' commented another. 'What a pretty bride he has!'

Wilberforce was all smiles and waved to everyone as he emerged from the church with Barbara on his arm. He was convinced that he was, that morning, easily the happiest man in England! He was thirty-eight years of age and Barbara was twenty.

'And where are you going to live, William?' asked a friend at the reception meal that followed his wedding.

'We are going to live at *Broomfield*,' said Wilberforce. 'It is a new house built on land adjacent to *Battersea Rise* where I have been living for quite a few years.'

'And where is *Battersea Rise*?' asked another guest.

'It is in the village of Clapham, just five miles south of London. It is a Queen Ann house with a beautiful oval-shaped library and with glass doors opening onto the lawn at the back. We have had some amazing people in recent years. Many of them love the Lord Jesus and are deeply committed to living godly lives in public service.'

'And what kind of people are they?' asked a person in the little group now gathered around Wilberforce.

'They are diplomats, legislators, businessmen and Members of Parliament. All are committed to the abolition of the slave trade. There is the Prime Minister's brother-in-law, James Stephen, Zachary Macaulay, the father of the famous historian, Thomas Macaulay, and John Venn, the Rector of Clapham Parish Church. They have been nicknamed 'The

Clapham Saints'.'

'I look on them as a group of pools which I am seeking to make into a river against slavery.'

It was, then, to *Broomfield* that William brought his new bride, Barbara.

One morning, early, in the year 1797 Wilberforce went into London and called at a very famous shop in the Strand. It belonged to a young man called Thomas Cadell who was a publisher. Wilberforce had in his hand the manuscript of a book which he had been writing for some time.

'Thomas,' he said to the publisher, 'I wonder would you be interested in publishing this book of mine? It sets out the essential Christian doctrines by Scripture texts and tries to show how far we are removed in England from what the New Testament teaches.'

'I don't think too many people would be interested in a religious book, Mr. Wilberforce,' said Cadell quietly, 'but if your name is on the book then I will print 500 copies.'

Thomas Cadell was soon to be surprised, for the publication became one of the most famous of its day. It went on to become a best seller and was translated into French, German, Italian, Spanish and

Dutch. It took its readers on a journey to discover how Christianity should and could guide the politics, habits, views and attitudes of everyone, and a copy was soon to be found in thousands of homes, including those of the poor.

All sorts of people were helped and blessed by it and it was used by God to reverse a huge slippage in behaviour and unbelief across Britain. John Newton called the book 'The most valuable and important publication of the present age.' No politician had ever written such a book before and no politician has written one since.

In the book Wilberforce particularly condemned the practice of duelling, a cruel method used for settling disputes of honour. A man who considered that he had been insulted felt that he could only restore his honour by calling a duel. He would send for two friends, called seconds, to challenge his opponent, who also appointed two seconds. The seconds would agree about the rules of the duel, and the challenger would choose a weapon. If the insult was only slight, one's honour would be satisfied by an exchange of shots or the infliction of a slight wound. If the insult was serious, the duel would be fought until one of the two fighters was killed or seriously wounded. Happily, duelling is now against the law.

A few mornings after Wilberforce had moved into the house at *Broomfield*, his secretary rushed into his room.

'Mr Wilberforce!' said the man. 'I am afraid I have to tell you some very frightening and sad news.'

'What is it Ashley?'

'It is about your friend Pitt.'

'And what on earth has he done?' asked Wilberforce.

'He has just had a duel with an Irish Member of Parliament called George Tierney.'

'I can hardly credit he would be so crazy to do such a thing,' replied Wilberforce, who was profoundly shocked. Unfortunately, the news was accurate.

At dawn, on Whit Sunday, 1798 a carriage had pulled up at an isolated spot on Putney Heath and out had stepped the Prime Minister and his friend Dudley Ryder. At the same time a hired coach arrived with George Tierney and his friend, George Walpole. Other carriages soon arrived carrying the Speaker of the House of Commons and two surgeons. Four cases of pistols were unstrapped and the seconds, Ryder and Walpole, began to talk and walk between Pitt and Tierney trying to bring peace between them.

'Would you not withdraw those fierce words you used in the House of Commons against the Prime Minister's war policy, Mr Tierney?' asked Ryder.

'Certainly not, Mr Ryder!' replied Tierney, 'I meant every word I said.'

'But you realise you could die if this duel takes place, Mr Tierney? Are words worth your life or the life of the Prime Minister?' asked Ryder.

'I will not withdraw my words,' said the huge Irish Member of Parliament.

Meanwhile George Walpole did his best to stop the Prime Minister.

'Why don't you just accept Mr Tierney's attack as merely a difference of opinion, Prime Minister?' said Walpole. 'This nation desperately needs you and it would be a tragedy if you lost your life. The nation needs you to lead it to victory over its real enemies.'

'I refuse to be reconciled to Tierney,' said Pitt. 'He insulted me and the work that I am doing in this nation. We must fight the duel.'

Pitt and Tierney were then placed at twelve paces from each other and the order was given to fire. Everybody standing there held their breath, including the Speaker of the House of Commons who watched from a horse.

'Thank God they missed,' breathed the Speaker, fully expecting the huge Tierney or the thin-as-a-pole Pitt to be lying in a pool of blood.

Another pistol was then handed to each man. Again they fired. This time, fortunately, Pitt fired into the air and to everybody's great relief, both escaped unhurt and the duellists returned to London in the same coach!

Wilberforce was not only shocked when he heard the news, he was furious. The duel became the talk of London and when Wilberforce got to Westminster he found everybody discussing it.

The Prime Minister's actions stung Wilberforce into action. He believed that duelling was a sinful practice and against the laws of God. How could a Prime Minister risk his very life over a quarrel which could have been solved without any risk to life? Wilberforce believed that Pitt had put his private feelings before duty to his country and to God. He immediately decided to introduce a Bill in Parliament to do away with duelling for ever.

It was not long before the Prime Minister reacted. He wrote to Wilberforce saying that if the Bill was passed he would have to resign as Prime Minister because he had been a duellist.

Once again the conflict between Wilberforce's Christian values and loyalty to his friend was not easy to handle.

With all his heart Wilberforce believed that Pitt was the very best national leader Britain could have and, on reflection, he felt it was not right to force his resignation for something which was lawful in the nation at that time.

He finally withdrew his Bill and it was a very grateful Prime Minister who wrote; 'How sincerely I feel your cordial friendship and kindness on all occasions, as well as when we differ as when we agree.'

The Prime Minister was mercifully alive to carry on a much more important fight which was soon to have England on the verge of invasion. The Grand Army of the French was massing at Boulogne and their Commander-in-Chief was watching the shores of England through a telescope and muttering; 'A favourable wind and thirty-six hours.'

His name was Napoleon Bonaparte.

'The purchase of slaves in Africa and their transport to the West Indies or any other country is hereby utterly abolished and declared illegal.'
4.am May 1st 1807.
Passed by 283 votes to 16

'It is the Lord who has done this, this is all a direct answer to our prayers. Without Him we could have done nothing.'
William Wilberforce

A Night of Nights

'It's Bonaparty! It's Bonaparty!' screamed little Laura Thornton who lived next door to William and Barbara Wilberforce.

Laura had gone to the stable loft before breakfast to visit a litter of puppies and had caught sight of a man's legs sticking out of the straw.

'Daddy! Daddy!' screamed Laura as she raced to the safety of her house. 'He'll kill me! He'll kill me!'

'Now Laura, it's hardly the Emperor of the French in our stable loft,' said her father, Henry Thornton.

'But it is! It is!' cried Laura, terrified, 'I have seen his boots sticking out of the straw!'

'All right, then, let's go and see if we can talk to the Emperor!' said Henry, heading immediately towards the stable loft.

Fortunately for everyone at *Battersea Rise*, the Emperor turned out to be only a groom fast asleep in the loft! Poor Laura had been told by her friends that if Napoleon and his army invaded England he would have all the children murdered in their beds. Her imagination had got carried away.

The threat of a French invasion, though, was very real. For months on end, Britain waited for the French to invade and all around the country Martello Towers were erected to enable lookouts to keep an eye on the coastline. Some of those towers still remain to this day.

'Do you think he will come, William?' asked Henry Thornton when telling Wilberforce the story of Laura's fright.

'I hear he has already gathered a corps of English speaking guides ready to act as interpreters when his army invades. He has actually had coins stamped with the words 'Invasion Of England'.'

'He has some nerve, then.'

'Indeed. He has also assembled a fleet of flat-bottomed boats to carry his troops across the English Channel, and has undertaken very complicated manoeuvres to make the British scatter their battleships and leave the Channel unprotected.'

'Will he win, William?' asked Henry, now feeling fear gripping his own heart.

'He reckons without the great Admiral, Lord Nelson,' replied his friend.

Wilberforce was right. It was Nelson who made sure that Napoleon never invaded England. Off a low headland near the entrance to the Straights of Gibraltar, Nelson fought a combined French-Spanish fleet at the Battle of Trafalgar on October 21st, 1805. There were twenty-seven British ships with two thousand one hundred and thirty-eight guns against the French-Spanish fleet of thirty-three ships and two thousand six hundred and forty guns.

The French ships were in a loose line formation when Nelson decided to split his fleet into two and drive them through the French line at different points. The Battle commenced at 12 noon after Nelson had given one of the most famous signals in history: 'England expects that very man will do his duty.'

At 1.30 pm. Lord Nelson was mortally wounded by a sniper's bullet.

By 3 pm. the battle was over and Nelson died a few hours later, but not before he knew that the defeat of the enemy was certain. Fifteen ships had been sunk, eighteen escaped, two were wrecked and four were captured later. The British lost no ships but four hundred and forty-nine British sailors were killed and one thousand two hundred and forty-two wounded. The French-Spanish fleet lost fourteen thousand sailors in the Battle.

It was a glorious time for England when on one November night in 1805 messengers galloped frantically along the Portsmouth Road, shouting news of the great victory.

'Look Barbara,' said Wilberforce, sadly, as he and Barbara stood on the streets of Yoxall in Staffordshire watching the stagecoaches rattling through.

'What do you see, William?' asked his wife.

'Every stagecoach has evergreens on it for Trafalgar and black crepe commemorating the death of Lord Nelson.'

'It is so tragic that Lord Nelson had to lose his life after such a glorious victory,' said Wilberforce, 'but at least Napoleon's command of the seas is now at an end. He will have to concentrate on fighting on land.'

Nelson was buried at St Paul's Cathedral and a great column and statue were erected to his memory at Trafalgar Square in London. His flagship, 'HMS Victory' can still be seen at Portsmouth.

The Napoleonic wars killed more than Lord Nelson. Wilberforce always maintained that they also killed his best friend, William Pitt.

One frosty December night while Pitt lay very ill, the British Foreign Secretary arrived in haste with some very important dispatches for him.

'What has happened that you should travel the distance to Bath to see me, my Lord Castlereagh?' asked Pitt.

'There has been a huge victory by Napoleon at Austerlitz in Austria, Prime Minister,' replied the Foreign Secretary. 'Napoleon, has taken Vienna and gone on to defeat the combined armies of our allies, Russia and Austria, at Austerlitz. He has inflicted huge casualties. The Austrians have signed a treaty with Napoleon, and the Russian Army has retired to its own borders.'

'Bring me a brandy and a map of Europe,' said Pitt, 'and leave me alone.'

As the Prime Minister read the dispatches and studied the map of Europe he knew that the Emperor Napoleon was now the ruler of the Continent. He knew that it would be a very long time before any army could defeat him. Deeply depressed, the Prime Minister sent for a servant.

'You called, Prime Minister,' said the servant.

'Roll up that map,' said Pitt. 'It will not be needed these ten years.'

The burden of it all became too much for William Pitt and on January 21st, 1806, within one month of hearing the news of Austerlitz he died, murmuring, 'My country, how I leave my country!' He was 46 years of age.

Wilberforce was heartbroken that a friendship which had lasted for thirty years was now at an end. At the request of Pitt's family, he helped to carry the Banner of the Crest of the late Prime Minister in the funeral procession up the aisle at Westminster Abbey.

Later, when Pitt was criticised in the House of Commons for the way he had handled the war, Wilberforce rose to defend his memory;

'A man must not be judged wholly by his success or failure and in war, above all, many unforeseen things happen. I have always admired and esteemed him for his great talents, his exalted character and patriotism ... no man ever loved his country with a warmer or more sincere affection.'

'Ah! William!' said Lord Grenville, Pitt's cousin, who had now become British Prime Minister on Pitt's death, 'do you remember how we three sat under the oak tree at Pitt's home in Kent and decided to fight the slave trade?'

'I certainly do,' replied William, 'and despite these frightening days of war I have not forgotten their cause.'

Wilberforce had been recently heartened to find that men in Parliament were really determined to abolish the slave trade. When the Secretary of State, James Fox, moved for a Bill similar to the one he had tried, again and again, to get through, he was thrilled.

It was to be finally decided on the night of 23rd February 1807. Wilberforce entered the House of Commons on that evening to find it unusually full of members.

To his great surprise, speech after speech complimented him and supported the Bill. Enthusiasm for Wilberforce's cause was very evident and it came to a head when the Solicitor General, a man called Romilly, made an impassioned speech, comparing Wilberforce's life with Napoleon's. Napoleon had brought great bloodshed but Wilberforce, great blessing.

Romilly's speech ended to the 'Hear! Hear!' of the delighted Members of Parliament. Almost every man was on his feet, turned towards Wilberforce and chorusing: 'Hip Hip Hooray!'

Wilberforce was so overcome, he simply sat with his head bowed and tears pouring down his face. It turned out to be the greatest night of his political life.

At 4 am. a vote was taken and the Bill was passed. It stated that, after May 1st, 1807, 'The purchase of slaves in Africa and their transport to the West Indies or any other country is hereby utterly abolished and declared illegal.' It was passed by 283 votes to 16.

From that moment it would be illegal for anyone in Britain to take part in the slave trade.

Wilberforce now went immediately to his London house at 4 Palace Yard, and his friends flooded in to congratulate him.

'For he's a jolly good fellow, and so say all of us,' they sang.

'It is the Lord who has done this,' said Wilberforce, 'this is all a direct answer to our prayers. Without Him we could have done nothing.'

'Let's name the sixteen miserable Members who voted against the Bill,' said a politician called William Smith.

'Never mind the miserable sixteen,' laughed Wilberforce, 'let us think of our glorious two hundred and eighty-three!'

On March 25th, 1807, the King gave his assent and the Bill for the Abolition of the Slave Trade became law. Amid all the congratulations and euphoria William Wilberforce knew that he had fulfilled only part of his great task. He now turned to the task of seeking to abolish the slavery that still continued in the British Dominions. While it was now illegal for British people to be involved in the purchase and transportation of slaves, people in British Dominions abroad still held the slaves they had already purchased. Would Wilberforce and his friends be able to free them?

Mrs Henson's freedom was closer than she realised.

'Oh, Lord Jesus, how
long? How long shall
I suffer this way?'
Mrs Henson,
Slave

July 31st, 1834.
Eight hundred thousand slaves
in the West Indies set free.

Free at Last

William Wilberforce was now easily, one of the most famous and respected men in his nation. In charge of a committee of sixty-nine Societies, as well as carrying his responsibilities in the House of Commons, the strain of having to constantly travel in and out of London was getting too much.

'What about moving to London, Barbara?' he asked, one day. There is a suitable house for sale in Kensington Gore.'

'What do you particularly like about it, William?'

'Well, it has a veranda and three acres of garden and fine old trees. The children will have plenty of room to play.'

The Wilberforces now had six children; William, Barbara, Elizabeth, Robert Isaac, Samuel, and the new baby, Henry. They eventually moved to Kensington House, their new home and were delighted with it.

Wilberforce was never happier than when he was in the company of children. He ran races with them, played lots of games and loved to read to them. One little girl later wrote of him: 'He was as restless as a child and during the long and grave discussions that went on between him and my father and others in the library, he was most thankful to refresh himself by throwing a ball or a bunch of flowers at me, or opening the glass doors and going off with me for a race on the lawn to warm his feet. I must never disturb Papa, but it didn't matter disturbing Mr Wilberforce.'

Lots of people disturbed Mr Wilberforce. Visitors to London today might be very surprised to discover that when they pass through the entrance hall of the famous Royal Albert Hall, they are almost on the site of William Wilberforce's former London home.

After breakfast all kinds of people began calling, asking for his advice, and some begging for his money. Few were refused.

'Factories did not spring up more rapidly .... than schemes of benevolence (kindness) beneath his roof,' said one observer. So crowded was his house any mid-morning that one of his aides had to go from group to group trying to find out 'who was begging for what.' Then Wilberforce would move quickly from group to group, bringing up his eyeglass as he listened, sympathised or pitied.

One of the most fascinating things ever accomplished by Wilberforce was completed at this time of his life. For a long time he had been concerned that British Government had been opposed to giving permission to Christian missionaries to work in India. This was mainly because they felt that trouble between the various religions would come as a result of the spread of the Gospel. They wanted to avoid any religious rioting at all costs.

'But the thing is ridiculous,' Wilberforce would say at his dinner table. 'Listen to this list of names!' He would then read out the names of women who had recently died in India through a practice called 'suttee.' This practice consisted of Hindu widows burning themselves alive on the fire that cremated their husband's dead body.

'But can you really stop it?' people would ask him.

'The Christian Gospel could stop it, if only they would let it loose across India,' Wilberforce would reply, gently yet with great confidence.

He did his best to get the Church of England to do something about it and led a deputation to see the new British Prime Minister, Spencer Percival, about the matter.

'I am in great sympathy with you Mr Wilberforce,' said the Prime Minister who was a committed Evangelical Christian, 'I will do my best to help.'

Wilberforce and his deputation left Downing Street greatly heartened that he would help them stop so many needless deaths.

'William, have you heard the news?' said a friend shortly after Wilberforce had been to see the Prime Minister.

'No, what is it? Is something wrong?'

'It is an absolute tragedy, William. The Prime Minister has been murdered in the lobby of the House of Commons. They tell me he was shot by a man called John Bellingham, a merchant from Liverpool. Bellingham blames Government policy for ruining his business.'

'I am so sorry,' said Wilberforce, 'the Prime Minister was a good Christian man and it is a shame that his life has been cut off so quickly.'

The next Prime Minister was a man called Lord Liverpool. Wilberforce approached him with the same enthusiasm regarding missionaries for India. He also started a huge campaign of public petitions which were sent to the Government on the matter.

On the night of June 22nd, 1813, Wilberforce rose to a packed House of Commons to plead for freedom to allow the Gospel to be spread in India. He held his audience enthralled for three hours.

Amazingly, Parliament responded with enthusiasm and voted in full favour of liberty to be given for the spread of the Christian Gospel in India. All the subsequent work done by Christian missions in India owe their opportunity to William Wilberforce who had, by God's help and guidance, been used to turn the key to open the door.

But what of his greatest cause? What would the freedom fighter do now? The answer was he would do all he could to banish slavery from the face of the earth. He worked for weeks on a long letter to the Tsar Alexander of Russia, encouraging the abolition of slavery.

The Tsar was in London on a visit and sent for Wilberforce. He was one of the most powerful men in all of Europe at that time and it was a great honour to be invited to meet him.

Wilberforce wondered how on earth he would be able to talk to the great man of Europe. He was very relieved to discover that the Tsar spoke to him in French, which Wilberforce could understand very well.

On the other hand, Wilberforce was not able to speak French easily and was again very relieved to find that the Tsar could understand English, though he could not speak it easily! So the Tsar spoke in French and Wilberforce in English and they got on famously.

'I am so delighted to meet you, Your Excellency,' said Wilberforce, nervously.

'Your fame has gone before you, Mr Wilberforce,' answered the Tsar, 'I understand that you are very keen to see the slave trade abolished. I, too, detest what is going on.'

'I am very sorry to have to say, Your Excellency, that according to my research, in nearly four hundred years of the slave trade, fifteen million slaves have been delivered to buyers and some forty million

Africans have died while crossing the Atlantic.'

'It is incredible, Mr Wilberforce,' answered the Tsar, sadly. 'What would you really like me to do?'

'I would like you to encourage the French to get out of the slave trade. As you know we have already had it abolished here in Britain and I am hoping that soon we shall have it banned in the British Dominions.'

'I will do my very best,' answered the Tsar, 'we must get them to stop as quickly as we can.'

Before the Debate in the House of Commons on the coming Peace Treaty with France, Wilberforce and others got over a quarter of a million signatures petitioning Parliament to force the French to stop their slave trading. Again, they won the day.

* * * *

'Can you believe the news?' said Wilberforce, rushing in to dinner at his home one evening in 1814, 'Bonaparte has escaped from imprisonment on the island of Elba! He has raised an army in France once more.'

'Do you think he will win all his battles again?' asked Wilberforce's son, Samuel.

'This time he has to face the 'Iron Duke', Wellington, Samuel. I certainly hope that the British Army under Wellington and our allies get rid of this man once and for all!'

Strange as it may seem one of the very first Decrees that Napoleon made when he returned from the island of Elba was the Total Abolition of the French Slave Trade. He was finally defeated, at the great battle of Waterloo in 1815, and was exiled to the Island of St Helena in the Indian Ocean.

When the Monarchy was restored to France the French Slave Trade was made illegal in 1818. By now America, Denmark, and Sweden had declared slavery illegal and Spain and Portugal soon followed.

'The problem is, Mr Wilberforce,' said Fowley Buxton, a young friend of Wilberforce's who was also a Member of Parliament, 'it is one thing to make laws but it is quite another to make people obey them. All these countries that are now declaring slavery illegal are not enforcing the law against it.'

'Well, Fowley,' answered Wilberforce, 'at least Britain is enforcing her slavers to obey. If any British ship is found involved in the slave trade, a fine of one hundred pounds per slave on board is enforced, the captain will be transported for life to Australia and the ship will be confiscated to the British Crown.'

'But we must make it unlawful to own slaves in any British Dominion, Mr Wilberforce,' said Buxton. 'We must ensure that all slaves in any Dominion are set free.'

'That, my dear Fowley, is the crusade that I want you now to lead,' said Wilberforce. 'I want you to be the new main voice against slavery in the House of Commons. My health is beginning to deteriorate and I don't have the strength to keep on the front line of this battle.'

Sadly, it was true, and Wilberforce spoke for the last time in the House of Commons on 11th June 1824. His theme? Slavery.

He retired to the Highwood Hill Estate in Hendon, just outside of London in 1825. He kept up a fairly rigorous routine in his last years on earth.

Daily he rose at 7 am. and spent an hour in prayer and Bible study. At 9.30 am. he read prayers to his family and servants and at 10.30am. he had breakfast. He still answered many letters and walked in his garden before dinner at 5 pm.

During the evening he liked to read

aloud to his family and friends. He would often talk long into the night with any guests who were staying with him.

In 1827 he visited Hull, the place of his childhood, for the last time.

'Look at No.27,' he said as he went up the High Street. 'It is just as nice as ever it was in the days when I played with Sarah. How I miss my mother and father and sister. What a day we had here when they roasted the ox to celebrate my 21st birthday and my election to Parliament!'

Wilberforce's last public speech in April 1833 was at a meeting against slavery in Maidstone, Kent, part of a huge campaign which his friend Buxton was now waging.

As he spoke, a streak of sunlight invaded the Town Hall and old Wilberforce, now feeble and very frail, said with a gleam in his eye; 'The object of our long struggle is bright before us, the light of heaven beams on us, and is an earnest of our success.'

One week later he became ill and it was decided to take him to London to consult a doctor. Friends lent him their house at Cadogan Place.

As it happened he arrived just as the Bill to Abolish Slavery in the British Dominions was being debated in the House of Commons.

'I would give anything to be able to go and hear the Debate,' he said, 'but the plain fact is I can no longer walk.'

'But I will allow you out for ten minutes to let good fresh air into your lungs,' said Wilberforce's physician, Dr Chambers. 'Get out in your wheelchair for a little while before prayers and breakfast and then you can receive your friends later in the morning.'

One of those friends was William Ewart Gladstone who was to become British Prime Minister four times.

'Went to breakfast with old Mr Wilberforce,' Gladstone wrote in his diary, 'heard him pray with his family. Blessing and honour are upon his head.'

'Mr Wilberforce!' said his friend Tom Macaulay as he rushed in to see Wilberforce late one Friday evening. 'The Abolition of Slavery Bill has passed its Third Reading in the House of Commons. There is no question that the House of Lords will vote in favour of it. The Government are prepared to pay the West Indian plantation owners twenty million pounds in order to free their slaves.'

'Thank God,' said Wilberforce, 'that I have lived to witness a day in which England is willing to give twenty million sterling for the Abolition of Slavery.'

The thrill that the old campaigner received at the news was incalculable.

At 3 am. three days later, on Monday, July 29th, 1833, William Wilberforce went to be with the Lord.

* * * *

The death of William Wilberforce brought immense feeling across Britain.

Within hours of his death two letters, signed by the Lord Chancellor and the Duke of Gloucester, and by many Members of Parliament and Peers from the House of Lords were sent to ask his family to permit burial at Westminster Abbey. There was a huge attendance as the choir sang and tributes were given to one of the greatest Christian lives Britain has ever known. The huge practical effect of his life was seen one year later on July 31st, 1834, when eight hundred thousand slaves in the West Indies were set free.

Among them were families like the Hensons, whom we first met at the beginning of this book.

'Oh, Lord Jesus, how long?' Mrs Henson had prayed, 'how long shall I suffer this way?' The splitting up and ruin of countless families over the years through slavery was one of the darkest sins this world has ever known.

The man from Hull had become a major part of the answer to her prayer. By his dedicated and determined campaign against slavery he had fought and won an incredible victory for freedom.

The friend of slaves had died and gone to his richly deserved reward in Heaven, but the memory of his life and huge achievement is still near us, pointing upward.

*He upholds
the cause of the oppressed
and gives food
to the hungry.
The Lord sets prisoners free.
Psalm 146:7*

*In my anguish
I cried to the Lord,
and he answered
by setting me free.
Psalm 118:5*

Thinking Further Topics

You can use these Thinking Further Topics on your own or as part of a group. If you are part of a youth group you can use this book as a discussion starter. Try reading it together and then meeting afterwards to discuss the story and go through the topics.

These topics help you to think for yourself. They make the story not just something that happened in the past but something that will help you think about your life and your future.

Thinking Further Topics: 1.
A Letter From a Schoolboy

William Wilberforce was not always the well-known politician and freedom fighter. What was the name of the town in which he was born? What was this town famous for? William wanted to travel the world as a sea captain but God had other plans for him.

We all have plans for our lives. Do you have plans for your life? What would you like to be when you leave school? Perhaps you have plans for next weekend? Maybe you plan to get married one day, have a house, own a car... there are lots of things that people plan for - they don't always happen though and sometimes that is for the best.

God knows the future. He knows the past. He is eternal and all powerful. Our plans mean nothing compared to his plans. 'The plans of the Lord stand firm for ever,' Psalm 33:11 This is why it is important to include God in your plan making. Ask him for his opinion. Listen to what he says to you through his word, the Bible. Ask him to direct you in the right way - even if it means that it's not exactly the way you wanted to go in the first place. We can always ask people for advice. Sometimes it's good to consult an adult or our best friend. The Bible says that we should 'Make plans by seeking advice.' Proverbs 20:18. The best advice comes from God. We can always trust him. Proverbs 3:5-6. Even when something doesn't quite work out the way we had planned we should trust in God - he knows what is best. His plans for us are good plans. Jeremiah 29:11.

Thinking Further Topics: 2.
To Cambridge

William was very intelligent. As a young man he went to university to study but he didn't work that hard. He would quite often waste his time in fooling and joking about. William preferred mimicing people and entertaining his friends to having his nose in a book. But what happened when the exam results came back? He had passed but he knew he could have done a lot better.

What do you think when you see someone who is obviously talented but who wastes their gift either by not bothering to use it or by using it in a wrong way? Can you think of stories in the news where a talented or famous person has misused their talents or gifts?

What about you? Can you think of times when you have wasted your talents? Perhaps you think that this doesn't concern you as you are not a top class football player or a brilliant mathematician. But talents and gifts can mean lots of things. Write down some things you think you are good at or that you enjoy doing. Ask God to show you how to use these gifts for his glory. We are given many gifts from God. Here are just a few: Time, friends, money, family, home, school, health. The most important gift God has given us is, of course, his Son, Jesus Christ. We can have forgiveness from our sins when we trust in him. Jesus Christ gave up his life so that we can live. We have been given many gifts. Read the following verse: Luke 12:48. Write it out on a piece of card and put it in your wallet or stick it on your fridge. Do the same for this verse: 'Thanks be to God for his indescribable gift.' 2 Corinthians 9:15.

Thinking Further Topics: 3.
The Shrimp who Swelled into a Whale

William Wilberforce became a politician. When people saw him first stand up to speak at a political meeting they didn't think he would be anything spectacular. But they soon changed their minds. Do you dream of being something like a writer or an astronaut? Maybe one day you will be in the history books along with William Wilberforce.

But are you in God's book? If you are in God's book of life and trust Jesus - you are in God's family. That is the most important thing. One day God may use you to do great things for him. If he does, remember that it is God who is behind it all. He is in charge. Give the glory to him. It is his by right.

But stop for a minute and look up the following verses in the Bible: 1 Corinthians 1:27; Isaiah 55:8-9. God's ways are not our ways and his thoughts are not our thoughts. We might long to do spectacular things for God but often it can be the ordinary jobs that are more important. These jobs may not get recognition from other people but God sees things done in secret. Matthew 6:6.

Some people pray for friends or relatives for years without telling anyone. It's a secret between them and God. Prayer is very important thing. Remember what it says in Matthew 6:6. Too often people think that prayer is not an important job, that it's not really 'doing' something. But prayer is talking to God - it helps us to know him better. Praying to God is obeying him and praying to God about a problem means that we are asking God to take control. We realise that he is the strongest - he will show us the way. 1 Corinthians 1:25.

154

Thinking Further Topics: 4.
Oh Happy Day

William Wilberforce was not always a Christian. He came to a point when he realised that he was not a Christian and started to try and find out how to become one. Maybe you think you are a Christian if your parents are Christians? Do you think being a Christian depends on what country you were born in or is it something deeper than that? A Christian is someone who belongs to Jesus Christ. So how does somebody belong to Jesus Christ? In Wilberforces time people belonged to other people when they were bought as slaves - but then many were ill-treated. When you belong to Jesus Christ you are not ill-treated - infact it is exactly the opposite because he loves you.

When you come to Jesus Christ and ask him to forgive your sins - you belong to him. He has bought you, but he didn't buy you with money... he bought you with his own blood. Do you find that difficult to understand? Read the following verses. Acts 20:28; 1 Corinthians 6:20. Jesus Christ died on the cross to take our punishment. We deserve the punishment of eternal death and Hell because of our sins - even the little disobediences that we do every day. Jesus however has never sinned so he agreed to take our punishment instead. If it had been left to us to take our own punishment no one would have survived. But Jesus, because of his perfect life, conquered death and came back to life. Now if you ask Jesus to take control of your life and forgive you, you become one of his people, for ever. Instead of belonging to death - those who believe in Jesus belong to him and he gives them life. John 3:16.

Thinking Further Topics: 5.
Amazing Grace

When you think about great and famous Christians like William Wilberforce and John Newton, does it make you feel inadequate? Do you think, 'I'll never do such amazing things for God.' Remember who the amazing one really is. What was that famous hymn that John Newton wrote? Who is it then who is really amazing? Read this hymn again. How does it describe God as amazing. Ask God to show you every day how amazing he really is.

If you are loving and trusting God and seeking to live your life as he would have you live it you may actually be doing great things for Jesus without even realising it. Read the following passage: Matthew 25:34-40.

Did you realise that when you do a kind deed or help someone even in a small way you are pleasing God? If you are a believer in God and do something for another believer it is as if you were actually doing that good deed for Jesus himself. What a privilege!

William Wilberforce did great things for God and he is in the history books because of this. But this is what William Wilberforce actually said, 'It is the Lord who has done this, this is all a direct answer to our prayers. Without him we could have done nothing.'

Even the little things that we do to please God - we can only do them because God helps us. He is a very patient and loving God. We should not make ourselves to be more important than we are. Perhaps you feel like giving yourself a pat on the back when you do something good. Before you get too proud about it remember that it is God who is good and no one else. Mark 10:18.

Thinking Further Topics: 6.
The Truth about the Slave Trade

William Wilberforce fought against injustice. He battled against the tyranny of the slave trade. He stood up for the rights of others.

Do you think that this was a hard thing for him to do? What made it particularly hard for William? Who was he fighting against?

Why should we fight against injustice anyway? How do you know when something is right or wrong? These are difficult questions and you can think about them for hours and not get anywhere. The best place to find out about why we should do something and what is right or wrong is in the Bible.

Look up the following verses: Ephesians 6:12; Psalm 37:28; Psalm 33:5; Psalm 103:6; Isaiah 56:1; Proverbs 2:1-15; Psalm 10:2,14,17-18; Psalm 82:3. Think about what they say about injustice. What does this show us about God's feelings towards injustice? Think about how William Wilberforce stood up for what was right. Think about the ways that you too can stand up for justice in your community.

When you fight against evil and injustice it can be very difficult. You don't increase your popularity that way. Jesus spoke out against injustice and sin. He also made a lot of enemies. Just remember - the next time you have to speak out against something that isn't fair or is wrong and contrary to God's ways - God is supporting you. Trust in the Lord Jesus Christ. He will protect you and even give you the right words to say Matthew 10:19-20.

Thinking Further Topics: 7.
Mr Greatheart

As well as fighting against the 'odious' slave trade William Wilberforce spent a lot of his time fighting for what he called 'manners' - what we might call 'morals' today. What are morals? The dictionary describes morals as right or wrong conduct. William Wilberforce was concerned at the low morals prevalent in his society. Another word for low morals is sin. Sin enters every area of our lives. That is why we have to give our lives completely to God. When we do this he will help us to fight against the sin in our lives. William Wilberforce tackled the sin in his own life by asking God to forgive him and take control of his life. Once he had done this he longed for other people to know the same joy and relief that he felt. Being forgiven by someone is an amazing feeling. Have you ever been forgiven for something? Have you ever heard a story of someone who showed amazing forgiveness? God's forgiveness is even better than that as it is perfect and lasts for ever.

Some people say that the morals of our society are decreasing steadily. Do you think that? Do you see evidence for the fact that people care less about God than they once did - for example fifty to one hundred years ago? Or do you think that there hasn't been much change? What worries you most about the world that you live in? Where would you like to see change? Write these thoughts down and pray about them. But remember, before you go pointing the finger at somebody else's sin or even before you pray about wickedness and sin in your community deal with the sin in your own heart first. Matthew 7:1-5; Isaiah 30:15; Luke 13:3.

Thinking Further Topics: 8.
The Duel

William Wilberforce was a good friend. William Pitt, the Prime Minister at that time said in a letter to Wilberforce, 'How sincerely I feel your cordial friendship and kindness on all occasions, as well as when we differ as when we agree.'

They did disagree sometimes. But when they disagreed they did not let it brake up their friendship. The Bible has good advice about friendships and relationships. Ephesians 4:26 says 'Do not let the sun go down when you are still angry.' This is useful advice. It's good to try and sort out a squabble before it goes too far. The longer it lies unforgiven the harder it is to bring the squabble to an end.

The Bible has specific advice for specific relationships. Exodus 20:12 tells us to 'Honour your father and mother.' Look this verse up and find out what happens when you do honour them. Ephesians 6:4 gives advice to parents. John 15:12 tells us to love each other as Christ loves us. Read Romans 13:9. Here you are told to love your neighbour as yourself. Do human beings normally behave in this way? Do you ever manage to do this? It is difficult but with God's help we can try. We should always put God first in our lives, then other people and then put ourselves last. We are told in the Bible about some relationships that were bad and some that were good. We can all learn something from these people about how God wants us to behave with our families and other people. Look up the following examples and perhaps you can add one or two of your own: Philippians 4:2-3; Genesis 4:1-12; 1 Samuel 19:1-7; John 13:1-17.

Thinking Further Topics: 9.
A Night of Nights

William Wilberforce lived at a very turbulent time in history. There was civil unrest, wars and great poverty throughout Europe. What do you think this year or this century will be remembered for in the future? Do you think it will be remembered as a time of peace or violence, hope or despair?

In the Bible when the nation of Israel turned away from God, God punished them. He punished them for their own good so that they would turn back to him and away from evil. Do you think this might happen to your country? If so what can you do about it? Do you pray for your country and it's rulers. Read 1 Timothy 2:1-2. Make a note to pray regularly for those with national responsibilities. Pray for your Prime Minister or President.

If you worry about the future - think for a minute. God is in control! Read Isaiah 14:7. God has his plans and purposes. We can pray to him about world events, wars, famines, disasters - but trust God and his power. He knows everything and we don't. The Bible says that there will be 'wars and rumours of wars' Matthew 24:6. One day Jesus will come back again. This is a day to look forward to if you love and trust in him as your Saviour.

But when you do hear of frightening events on the news and see pictures of another battle or more refugees - read the following verses: Psalm 46:9-11. It doesn't matter what evil people try to do. They can never defeat God. He is so much bigger than them - so big that he can't be measured. In Psalm 37:13 we read that God even laughs at the wicked. So do not be afraid you can trust in God.

Thinking Further Topics: 10.
Free at Last

Try and imagine what it must have felt like to be a slave and then to be set free. What would someone like Mrs Henson have felt like when she realised that she and her child could be reunited? It must have been an amazing feeling - intense joy, disbelief, sadness too. Many slaves, though set free, never saw their homes or families again.

William Wilberforce was overjoyed too when the bill for the abolition of slavery was passed.

Slavery still exists in many countries today and on page 162 you can find out about Anti Slavery International who seek the abolition of slavery today.

But for a lot of us we already have freedoms which we take for granted. You have been given the freedom to read the Bible. Many Christians in the world today are not allowed to read or own a Bible. Many can't even afford to buy one.

We also have the freedom to learn, to read books, to make decisions, to vote. But real freedom comes from believing in Jesus Christ. John 8:36 'So if the Son sets you free you will be free indeed.' Read Romans 6:18 to find out what it is that Jesus frees us from. If you think about it you can be in prison, behind bars and yet if you love Jesus you are free in the best way - you are free from sin.

Pray for those Christians round the world who are in prison because they believe in Jesus and want to worship him. Thank God for the freedoms he gives you every day. If you have not asked him to free you from your sin, ask him to do this now. It will be the best freedom you ever have!

BOOKS FOR FURTHER READING

Uncle Tom's Cabin, Harriet Beecher Stowe
(Description of the life of a slave in America)
Wilberforce: The Nation's Conscience,
Patrick Cormack (Pickering)
Wilberforce, John Pollock (Lion Publishing)
The Water Babies, Charles Kingsley
(Description of the life of a boy chimney sweep)

PLACES TO VISIT

Wilberforce House
Britain's first slavery museum, High Street, Hull. Birthplace
of William Wilberforce. Display on the life of the slave
trade and the campaign to ban it.
*Open Monday - Saturday 10 am. - 5 pm.; Sunday 1.30
pm. - 4.30 pm.*

Transatlantic Slavery Exhibition
Maritime Museum, Albert Dock, Liverpool. This is a
fascinating exhibition where children can follow a fictional
slave through his experiences. Children can also board a
reconstructed slave ship.
Monday - Sunday; 10 am. - 5 pm. (Last admission 4 pm.)

WORTH SUPPORTING

'Anti-Slavery International', Stable Yard, Broomgrove Road, London SW9 9TL.
(An organisation seeking to eliminate slavery in all forms through research, awareness-raising, lobbying, public campaigning, and supporting like-minded organisations abroad and in the United Kingdom).
The International Labour Organisation states that there are 250 million child workers in the world today. 120 million of these children are forced to work full-time.

My Prayer Diary

The Bible says, 'Devote yourselves to prayer, being watchful and thankful. And pray for us, too' Colossians 4:2-3.

In this section here write down the names of those people you want to pray for every day. They may be your family and your special friends.

My Family and Friends.

Write down the names of your minister or church leader and those people who help him like Sunday School teachers, Youth workers etc.

Now write down the names of any people who especially need your prayers. They may be missionaries working overseas, or people doing other difficult jobs. Or they could be people who are old or ill or who are feeling lonely. Write down one person for every day of the week and pray for them every week on this day.

Sunday

Monday

Tuesday

Wednesday

Thursday

Friday

Saturday

After having read this book you should pray to God about some of the things you have learnt and about specific issues that have arisen throughout your reading.

Pray for those people who make the laws and decisions that effect you and your country.

Government

Thank God for the laws and decisions made in Government. Pray that these decisions will not go against God's law. Pray that more Christians will take part in Government and in the decision making that effects your nation.

National Leaders

Thank God for the leaders of your country. Ask him to bless them and to protect them. Pray to God that these men and women will come to know him and to love him. Pray for those who are Christians already. Thank God for them and the work they do. Pray that God will help them in their work and that they will be able to stand up and be counted as followers of Jesus Christ.

Write down the name of your Prime Minister or President, Member of Parliament or Representative in Government. Pray for them regularly.

Pray for your country and the other countries and tribal communities that make up your world

Your Country

Thank God for living in a free country, if you do. Ask him to bring revival to the Christians of this nation. Pray to God that he will bless your country and that the people will respect and glorify him.

If you do not live in a free country pray that God will reveal himself to your national leaders. Pray for them - that they will be brought to love and respect God. Thank God for the freedom he gives all believers through his Son, Jesus Christ.

Your World

Pray for other countries throughout the world. Pray for ogranisations such as Wycliffe Bible Translaters, OMF or Operation Mobilisation who are seeking to spread God's word throughout the world.

Pray for people throughout the world who are persecuted if they believe and worship Jesus Christ. Pray for their freedom. Thank God for their bravery. Pray for those countries where persecution takes place and for the leaders and people who persecute these believers. Pray that they will repent of their sin and come to the Lord Jesus Christ.

Pray specifically. Be informed about your world and nation.

Specific Issues

If you read a newspaper or watch the news remember to pray about national and world events. Pray about what is happening in your world today. Thank God that he is in control and take all your worries and concerns to him.

Pray about moral issues that are discussed in the media. Pray that Christians will be called apon to give God's point of view.

Pray that you too will be able to state clearly what it is that God thinks about sin. Ask God to prepare you to speak out for him. Ask him to teach you through his word, the Bible.

Injustice

Pray about any area where you see injustice. Ask God to show you how you can make a difference. Ask him to give you the courage to stand up for him and for his laws.

Pray for other Christians, pray for families and your family in particular.

Christian Church

Pray for the Christian Church. Pray that Christians will read God's word. Pray that the church will be active in fighting against sin and injustice and will turn back to God. Ask God to help Christians to obey him and his word and to put aside petty differences.

Christian Leaders

Pray for your own church leaders every day. Ask God to encourage them through his word, the Bible. Pray for those who preach from the Bible and who have been given the job of teaching Christians from God's word. Pray for those who have the job of teaching and looking after children. Thank God for all these people - and encourage them by thanking them for the work that they do.

Your Family

Pray for your family and for other families too. Pray that God will protect families. Pray that people will ask God to help them in their marriages and relationships.

A Voice In The Dark
Richard Wurmbrand

by Catherine Mackenzie

'Where am I? What are you doing? Where are you taking me?' Richard's voice cracked under the strain. His heart was pounding so hard he could hardly breathe. Gasping for air he realized - this was the nightmare! Thoughts came so quickly he could hardly make sense of anything.

'I must keep control,' he said out loud. An evil chuckle broke out from beside him. 'You are no longer in control. We are your worst nightmare!'...

When Richard Wurmbrand is arrested, imprisoned and tortured, he finds himself in utter darkness. Yet the people who put him there discover that their prisoner has a light which can still be seen in the dark - the love of God. This incredible story of one man's faith, despite horrific persecution, is unforgettable and will be an inspiration to all who read it.

ISBN 1-85792-298-0

From Wales to Westminster
Martyn Lloyd-Jones

by his grand-son
Christopher Catherwood

'Fire! Fire!' - A woman shouted frantically. However, as the villagers desperately organised fire fighting equipment the Lloyd-Jones family slept. They were blissfully ignorant that their family home and livelihood was just about to go up in smoke. Martyn, aged ten, was snug in his bed, but his life was in danger.

What happened to Martyn? Who rescued him? How did the fire affect him and his family? And why is somebody writing a book about Martyn in the first place? In this book Christopher Catherwood, Martyn's grandson, tells you about the amazing life of his grandfather, Dr. Martyn Lloyd Jones. Find out about the young boy who trained to be a doctor at just sixteen years old. Meet the young man who was destined to become the Queen's surgeon and find out why he gave it all up to work for God. Read about Martyn Lloyd-Jones. He was enthusiastic and on fire for God. You will be, too, by the end of this book!

ISBN 1-85792-349-9

The Watch-maker's Daughter
Corrie Ten Boom

by Jean Watson

If you like stories of adventure, courage and faith - then here's one you won't forget. Corrie loved to help others, especially handicapped children. But her happy lifestyle in Holland is shattered when she is sent to a Nazi concentration camp. She suffered hardship and punishment but experienced God's love and help in unbearable situations.

Her amazing story has been told worldwide and has inspired many people. Discover about one of the most outstanding Christian women of the 20th century.

ISBN 1-85792-116-X

The Storyteller - C.S. Lewis

by Derick Bingham

C.S.Lewis loved to write stories even as a small child. He grew up to face grief when his mother died, fear when he fought in the First World War and finally love when he realised that God was a God of love and that his son Jesus Christ was the answer to his heart ache.

C.S.Lewis brought this newly discovered joy and wonder into his writings and became known world-wide for his amazing Narnia stories.

Read all about this fascinating man. Find out why his friends called him Jack and not his real name. Find out what C.S.Lewis was really like and discover how one of the greatest writers and academics of the twentieth century turned from atheism to God.

"A good introduction to my stepfather
C.S. Lewis"
Douglas Gresham

by Catherine Mackenzie

Hudson Taylor is well-known today as one of the first missionaries to go to China but he wasn't always a missionary. How did he become one then? What was his life like before China? In this book you will meet the Hudson Taylor who lived in Yorkshire as a young boy, fell desperately in love with his sister's music teacher and who struggled to gain independance as a teenager. You will also travel with Hudson to the far east as he obeys God's call to preach the gospel to the Chinese people.

Witness the excitement as he and his sister visit London for the first time, sympathise with the heart-ache as Hudson leaves his family behind to go to China and experience the frustration as his sisters wait for his letters home.

Do you want to know more? Then read this book and let the adventure begin.

ISBN 1-85792-423-1

Look out for
the next in our

series:

George Müller

The children's
champion

written by

Irene Howat

 **CHRISTIAN FOCUS**

Good books with the real message of hope!

Christian Focus Publications publishes biblically-accurate books for adults and children.

If you are looking for quality bible teaching for children then we have a wide and excellent range of bible story books - from board books to teenage fiction, we have it covered.

You can also try our new Bible teaching Syllabus for 3-9 year olds and teaching materials for pre-school children.

These children's books are bright, fun and full of biblical truth, an ideal way to help children discover Jesus Christ for themselves. Our aim is to help children find out about God and get them enthusiastic about reading the Bible, now and later in their life.

**Find us at our web page:
www.christianfocus.com**